Student's Book

Pathway to Science 3

CB078505

Glue your picture here.

Name

Richmond

earch Skills

Example
A girl puts her head on the table and listens to the sound produced when her friend knocks on the other end of the table.
Why does the girl hear a noise when her friend knocks on the table?
The children answered: – You can hear a noise because knocking on the table produced vibrations.
The children plan to prove their answer with the following prediction: – If you put a plate of rice on one end of the table and knock softly on the other side, the plate will move.
In order to prove their hypothesis, the children do the following experiment. They find a plastic plate and put a little dry rice on it. They put the plate on one side of the table. Then they knock on the other side and observe what happens.
The children recorded their results as a drawing:

Before	After
	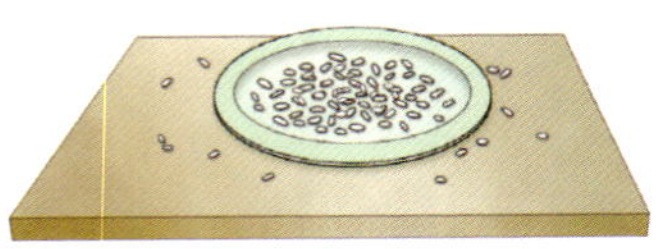

The rice scattered over the plate and onto the table because knocking on the table produced vibrations that moved the plate. So they know that the sound is produced by vibration.

What new research questions could you formulate after doing this experiment?

Richmond
58 St Aldates
Oxford
OX1 1ST
United Kingdom

Pathway to Science Student's Book Level 3

First Edition: 2014
Fourth Reprint: March 2015
ISBN: 978-607-06-0906-0

Pathway to Science 3 is a collaborative work, created and designed by the Department of Educational Research of Santillana.

Av. Río Mixcoac No. 274, Col. Acacias,
Benito Juárez, C.P. 03240, Ciudad de México

Publisher: Justine Piekarowicz
Editor: Dominic Wright
Art and Design Coordinator: Marisela Pérez
Pre-Press Coordinator: Daniel Santillán

Illustrations: Paula Gutiérrez Fischman, Marcelo Cáceres Ávila

Photographs: Jorge Quito Soto, César Vargas Ulloa
©REPOSITORIO: Editora Moderna, Ltda. (Brasil) p. 97;
©THINKSTOCK: iStock pp. 21 (pilipenkoD), 34 (John Beckman Jr), 40 (bdspn), 67 (Valua Vitaly), 90 (Mariakarabella), 95 (rifatp), 100 (Mariusz Świtulski), 110 (Mark Hatfield), 125 (alexokokok), 151 (jerryhopman), 154 (MagicDreamer), 155 (ManishMamtani), 157 (tomofbluesprings), 158 (DedMorozz), 163 (DENIS KHVESHCHENIK, szsz), 173 (GUIFANG HUANG); moodboard p. 67 (Mike Watson Images); Photodisc p. 157 (Photodisc); PhotoObjects.net p. 163 (PhotoObjects.net, Hemera Technologies); Stockbyte. pp. 34 (Jupiterimages), 110 (Stockbyte, John Foxx)
© C. Carreau/European Space Agency p. 124, Artist's view of Mercury
© NASA/JPL/University p. 125, Neptune
Cover Design: Erika Martínez
Cover Photograph: Máximo Ruiz, The Trifid Nebula

First published by Santillana del Pacífico S.A. de Ediciones

Printed in Brazil by Forma Certa Gráfica Digital
Lote: 792969
Cod: 292709060

How do plants reproduce?
What can we make out of trash?

One way to answer these questions is to use our:

Scientific Research Skills

They help us explain the phenomena around us.

You can use these skills when you are doing research projects and science labs!

We welcome you to explore and understand the skills you will use in different parts of the book. They will help you answer many questions about the world around you.

Come with us to discover a fun way to learn science!

	Scientific Res
	Process
Observe and Question	**Observation** You can **obtain information** about an object or a situation by using your five senses.
	Research Questions These come from observing a phenomenon or situation that can be explained by asking **questions**.
	Hypothesis This is an **anticipated answer** to your research question. It can be proved through experimentation.
	Predictions These are the **results** that you expect to obtain when researching the phenomenon or new situation.
Plan and Conduct an Investigation	**Experimental Procedure** This allows you to check or prove your hypothesis and your predictions through exploration and experimentation. In this stage, you gather **supplies** and follow a **procedure** to complete the experiment correctly.
	Results This is the data or information you obtain from experimenting and exploring. You can record and represent the results in various ways. For example, with drawings, diagrams, tables or graphs.
Analyze Evidence and Communicate	**Conclusions** These are the **central ideas** that you will find from analyzing the results. You will compare and contrast them with your hypothesis to verify it. Conclusions often allow you to formulate new research questions.

Introduction

Hi friends!

We are **Spot**  and **Kiki** , and we are here to welcome you to **Pathway to Science**. Follow this pathway to a very special place. Do you want to know why it is so special?

- It is full of magic, and everyone is welcome in it. You will find information, texts, pictures and activities presented in a simple and friendly manner. Here you will discover that learning is fun!
- This is a space where we can all learn to share and live together. The activities will help us reflect on our values and learn to respect others.
- It is open to people from all over the world, a place where you can continue to learn more and interactively with the help of the latest technology.

- It is filled with challenges that involve finding solutions, developing math skills and applying calculation strategies that you and your classmates will work on together.

We will be with you every step of the way!
All you need is curiosity and the desire to learn.

How is your textbook organized?

Pathway to Science 3 is organized into five units. Here is what you will find in each unit.

Initial Pages

- Number and title of the unit
- Learning objectives
- Initial evaluation

Organized into Sections

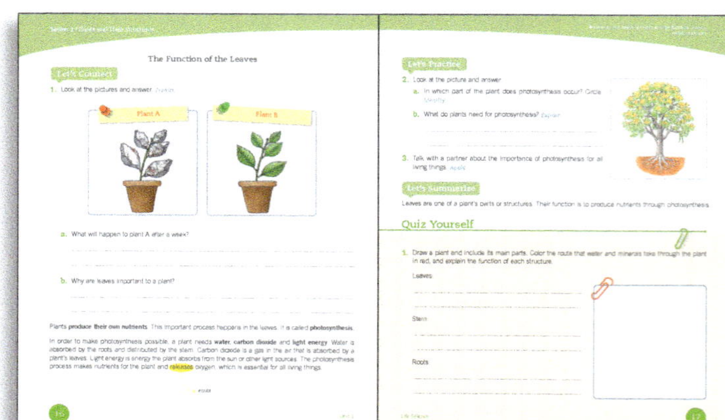

- Let's Connect
  Observe, read and answer
- Let's Explore
- Let's Practice
- Let's Summarize
- Quiz Yourself

Fun Features

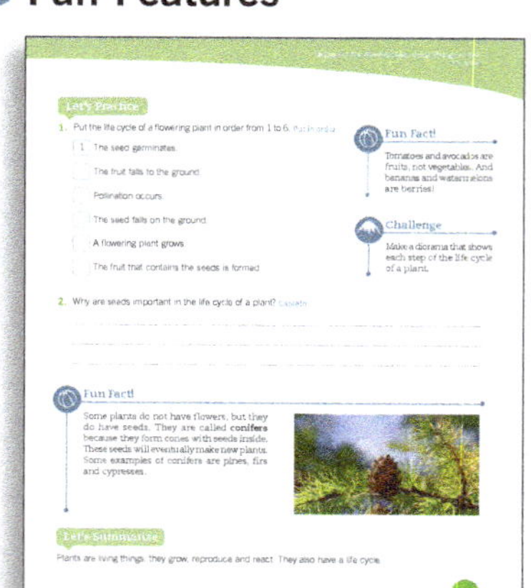

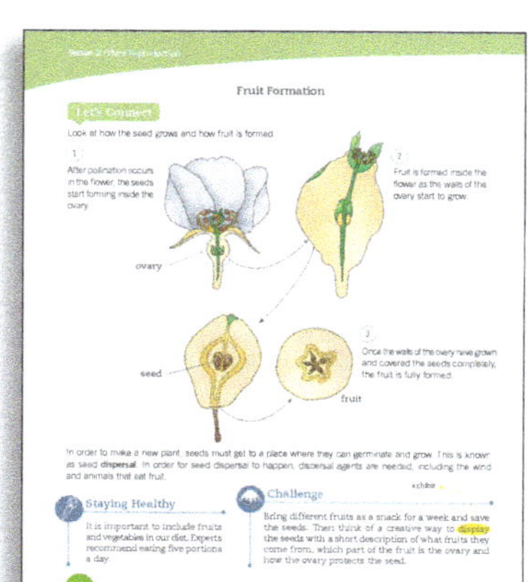

- Education through Values
- Staying Healthy
- Did You Know…?
- Remember!
- Tip
- Word Focus
- Fun Fact!
- Challenge

Evaluation Pages

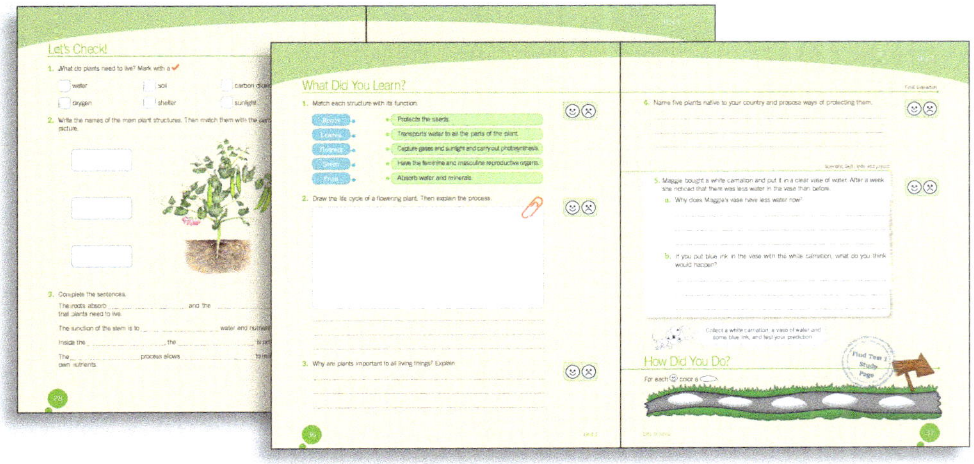

- What Do You Know?
  Initial Evaluation
- Let's Check!
  Intermediate Evaluation
- What Did You Learn?
  Final Evaluation

Special Pages

- Science Lab
- Test Study Pages
  Summary and Review to glue in your notebook

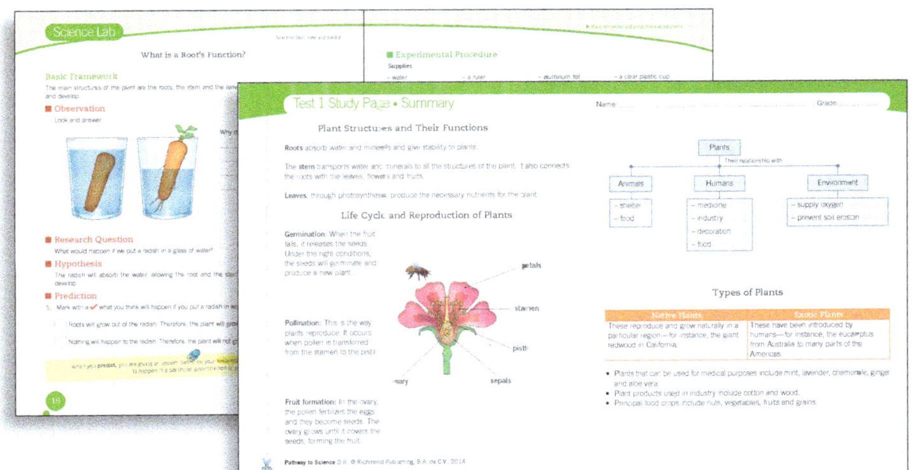

Support Pages

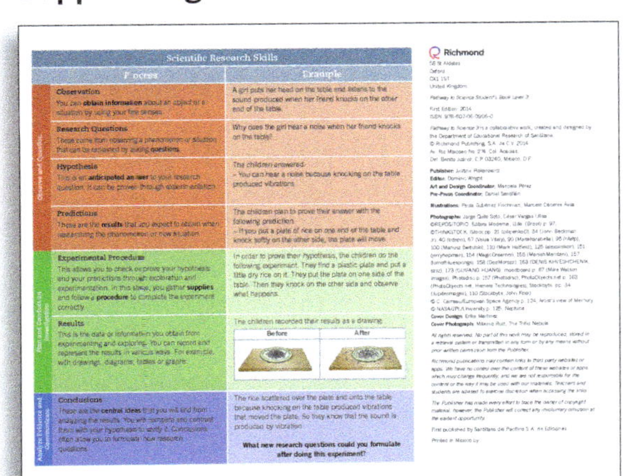

- Scientific Method Foldout
- Cutouts
- Activity Cards

Table of Contents

Unit 1

Plants

Key Words

native

life cycle

reproduce

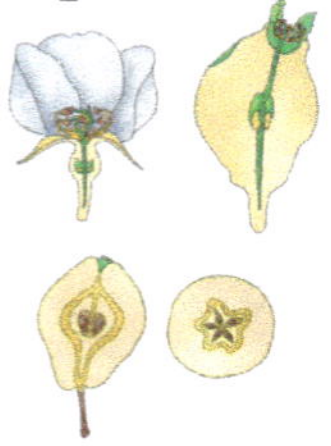

pollinate

crop

In this unit you will learn to:

- describe the needs of plants and the function of roots, stems and leaves.
- describe how flowering plants change throughout their life cycles.
- describe how plants are important to living things and the environment, and propose protection measures.
- identify different types of plants.
- make inferences and predictions about plants.
- value the importance of taking care of forests.

What Do You Know?

Initial Evaluation

1. Mark the plant characteristics with a ✔.

☐ They grow. ☐ They move. ☐ They react.

2. Classify the plants in the picture using the words below.

| tree | bush | grass |

3. What do plants need to live?

____

Scientific Skill: Infer and predict

4. Look at and describe the following pictures.

a. How is **plant 2** different from **plant 1**?

____

____

b. What would happen to **plant 1** if you cut its roots?

____

Section 1

Plants and Their Structures

Plant Structures and Needs

Let's Connect

1. Look at the picture and mark your answers with a ✓. Infer

When Mariana moved to a new house, she forgot to take out a plant her mother had put in a box. A few days later, she found it as shown in the picture.

a. What parts of the plant **withered**?

☐ roots ☐ leaves ☐ stem ☐ flowers

b. What was this plant missing in order to be healthy?

☐ air ☐ water ☐ light ☐ shelter

c. What does a plant need to live?

____

____

Plants have three main structures or parts: the **roots**, the **stem** and the **leaves**. Through their parts, plants receive the **water**, **light** and **air** that they need to grow. Some plants also have **flowers**, **fruits** and **seeds**.

Did You Know...?

Cacti are able to accumulate water because they have adapted to live in dry places. Ferns, on the other hand, need to live in humid environments.

Let's Practice

2. Write the names of the main parts of the plant. Identify

3. Match the parts of the plant with the labels that represent their needs. Relate

water

air

ice

light

wood

soil

Word Focus

Light

1. Not heavy.

2. The brightness produced by the sun, a lamp, a fire, etc.

How is it used in the text?

luminosity

Let's Summarize

Plants have three main structures or parts: the roots, the stem and the leaves. Through these, they get the water, light and air that they need to live.

The Function of the Roots

Let's Connect

1. Look at the pictures and answer.

Plant 1

Plant 2

a. What structures do you see in both plants? Identify

____

b. What differences do you see between the two sets of roots? Compare

____

____

c. Which plant's roots give it more support? Infer

____

____

The roots are the part of the plant that allow it to hold firmly to the ground and to absorb water and minerals that are essential for its development and growth. In this case, water and minerals go from the soil to the root.

Did You Know...?

long, thin, orange vegetable

Some plants, like carrots, have a very thick main root with other thinner roots coming from the thick one.

Let's Practice

2. Which of these roots will be able to absorb more water? Mark with a ✔. Predict

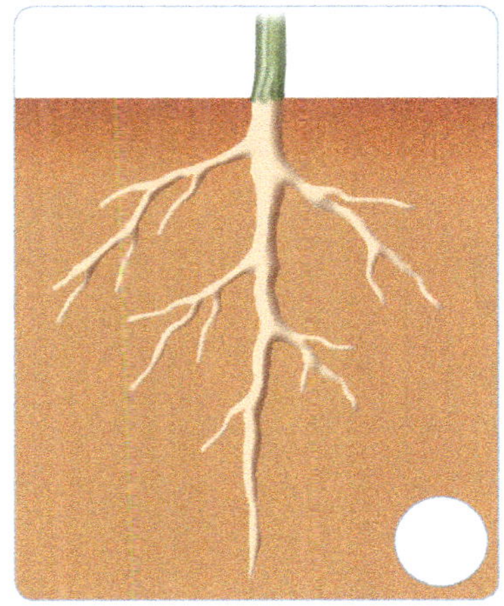

3. Explain what will happen in each situation. Predict

Situation 1

If you plant a carrot in a flowerpot with soil, will it grow?

→ small container for plants

____

____

Situation 2

If you plant a carrot in a flowerpot with **stones**, will it grow?

____

____

The roots grow in the opposite direction to the stem.

Let's Summarize

The function of a plant's roots is to absorb water and minerals and to stabilize the plant.

Staying Healthy

There are many roots that we eat on a daily basis, such as carrots and beets. These roots give us nutrients, such as vitamins and minerals, which help us grow and stay healthy. Do you know of any other edible roots? Research and find out!

→ beets: dark red root vegetable

The Function of the Stem

Let's Connect

1. Watch the two stages of an experiment carefully and answer. Infer

Material that does not let water go up the stem.

a. What differences can you find between situation 1 and situation 2?

____

____

b. Why did the water level not decrease in situation 2?

____

____

c. What is the stem for? Mark with a ✔.

☐ To absorb water and minerals.

☐ To transport substances to all the parts of the plant.

d. Which plant should have more water and minerals in its leaves at the end of the experiment?

____

The **stem's** function is to transport water and minerals absorbed by the roots to all the parts of the plant. It also connects the roots with the leaves, flowers and fruit.

Let's Practice

2. Karen wanted to prepare an experiment to show the function of a stem to her classmates. She found the following pictures.

Help Karen finish her assignment.

a. What materials does Karen need to do this experiment? Identify

____

b. Which steps should she follow in this experiment? Go to **Cutout 1** on **page 159** and glue the steps in the right order. Put in order

Let's Summarize

The main functions of the stem are to transport water and minerals and connect the parts of the plant.

The Function of the Leaves

Let's Connect

1. Look at the pictures and answer. Predict

a. What will happen to plant A after a week?

____

____

b. Why are leaves important to a plant?

____

____

Plants **produce their own nutrients**. This important process happens in the leaves. It is called **photosynthesis**.

In order to make photosynthesis possible, a plant needs **water**, **carbon dioxide** and **light energy**. Water is absorbed by the roots and distributed by the stem. Carbon dioxide is a gas in the air that is absorbed by a plant's leaves. Light energy is energy the plant absorbs from the sun or other light sources. The photosynthesis process makes nutrients for the plant and releases oxygen, which is essential for all living things.

releases → emits

Let's Practice

2. Look at the picture and answer.

a. In which part of the plant does photosynthesis occur? Circle. Identify

b. What do plants need for photosynthesis? Explain

____

____

3. Talk with a partner about the importance of photosynthesis for all living things. Apply

Let's Summarize

Leaves are one of a plant's parts or structures. Their function is to produce nutrients through photosynthesis.

Quiz Yourself

1. Draw a plant and include its main parts. Color the route that water and minerals take through the plant in red, and explain the function of each structure.

Leaves:

____

____

Stem:

____

____

Roots:

____

____

What is a Root's Function?

Basic Framework

The main structures of the plant are the roots, the stem and the leaves. Each one allows the plant to grow and develop.

Observation

Look and answer.

Why do you think the carrot grew?

____

____

____

____

When you **infer,** you are giving a possible answer based on an observation.

Research Question

What would happen if we put a radish in a glass of water?

Hypothesis

The radish will absorb the water, allowing the root and the stem to develop.

Prediction

If you want to better understand what **predict** means, look at the example in the **Scientific Research Skills** foldout.

1. Mark with a ✔ what you think will happen if you put a radish in water.

- [ ] Roots will grow out of the radish. Therefore, the plant will grow.
- [ ] Nothing will happen to the radish. Therefore, the plant will not grow.

When you **predict,** you are giving an answer based on your knowledge about what you think is going to happen in a particular phenomenon or process.

knowledge → learning

Experimental Procedure

Supplies

- water
- a radish
- a ruler
- a marker
- aluminum foil
- 2 skewers (a long piece of wood or metal)
- a clear plastic cup

Steps

1. With the help of an adult, cut the ends of the radish.
2. Push a skewer through each side of the radish. This will create a way to support the radish over the cup (see photograph 1). **Warning**: be careful when using the skewers.
3. Pour water into the cup until it covers the bottom of the radish. Mark the water level on the cup with the marker.
4. Cut a piece of foil and cover the top of the cup (see photograph 2).
5. After seven days, observe the water level and the bottom of the radish.
6. Write your observations in your notebook.

photograph 1

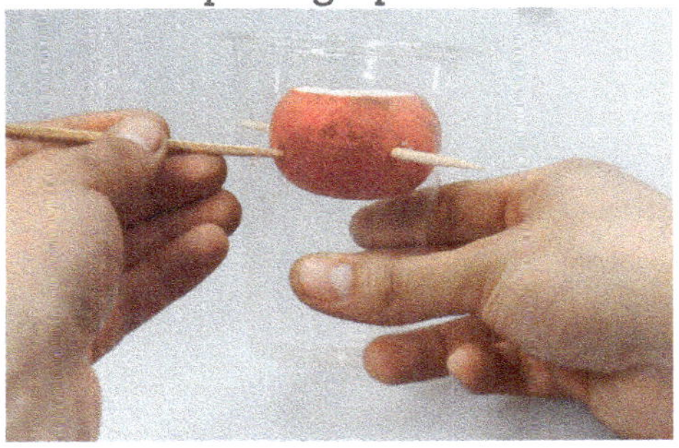

photograph 2

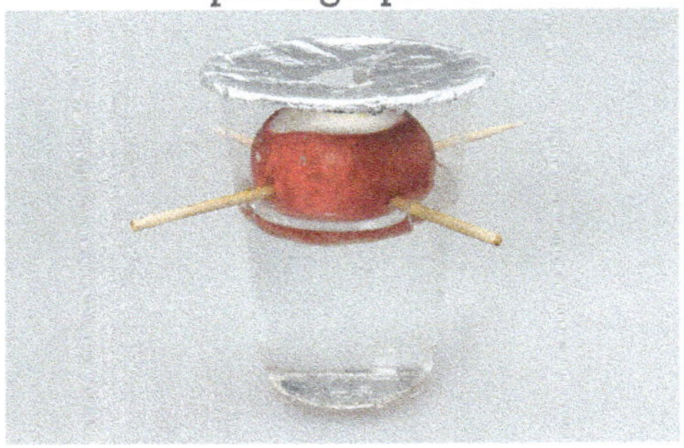

Results

1. Did the root grow? ☐ yes ☐ no
2. What happened to the water level?

   ☐ It increased. ☐ It decreased.

Conclusion

1. Was your prediction correct? ☐ yes ☐ no
2. According to your results, what is the main function of the root?

____

____

In this experiment, you **inferred** based on observation. The prediction allowed you to give an anticipated answer about what was going to happen to the radish if it was left in a cup of water.

Plant Reproduction

The Life Cycle of Flowering Plants

Let's Connect

As you already know, plants are living things: they grow, they reproduce and they react. Also, they experience a series of changes throughout their lives, which means they have a life cycle. Look at the life cycle of a flowering plant.

throughout: from the beginning to the end

When the fruit has developed seeds, it falls from the tree.

On the ground, the seeds are released and then **germinate**. This will allow a new plant to grow.

pollination: transfer of pollen from one flower to another

When a plant is fully developed, flowers appear. Flowers are involved in **reproduction**.

The pollination of the flower leads to the formation of fruits and seeds, and a new cycle begins.

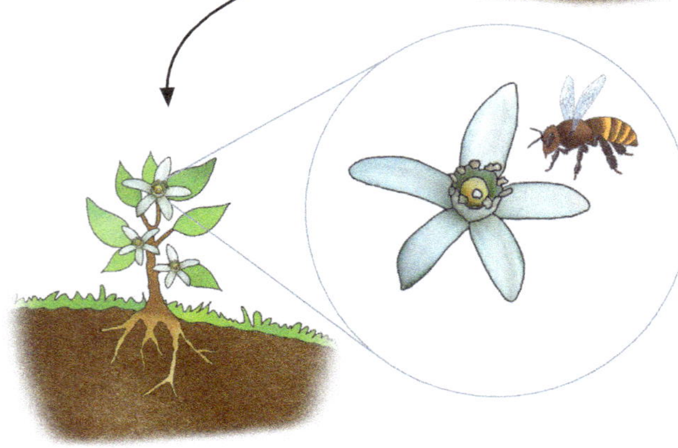

How do plants without flowers reproduce? Do some research!

Let's Practice

1. Put the life cycle of a flowering plant in order from 1 to 6. Put in order

- [1] The seed germinates.
- [ ] The fruit falls to the ground.
- [ ] Pollination occurs.
- [ ] The seed falls on the ground.
- [ ] A flowering plant grows.
- [ ] The fruit that contains the seeds is formed.

Fun Fact!

Tomatoes and avocados are fruits, not vegetables. And bananas and watermelons are berries!

Challenge

Make a diorama that shows each step of the life cycle of a plant.

2. Why are seeds important in the life cycle of a plant? Explain

____

____

____

Fun Fact!

Some plants do not have flowers, but they do have seeds. They are called **conifers** because they form cones with seeds inside. These seeds will eventually make new plants. Some examples of conifers are pines, firs and cypresses.

Let's Summarize

Plants are living things: they grow, reproduce and react. They also have a life cycle.

Seed Germination

Let's Connect

1. Look at the pictures of the results of an experiment. Infer

A bean seed that was watered.

A bean seed that was not watered.

watered: provided with water

a. Why did one of the seeds germinate?

☐ Because it was watered.

☐ Because it was not watered.

b. Which stage of the life cycle is being studied in this experiment?

☐ fruit formation ☐ germination

As you saw in the activity above, a seed can develop into a new plant. This process is called **germination**, and it happens when the outside of the seed breaks open and a new plant grows from it.

Some seeds are in a **latent period**, which means they are in an **inactive state** waiting for the right conditions to germinate. They need things like appropriate temperature and water and enough light, which vary according to the type of seed. Seeds can survive for long periods of time without germinating thanks to their protective shell.

survive: continue to exist

▲ The flowering desert phenomenon is an example of seeds after a latent period.

Let's Practice

2. A scientist was studying the germination process of seeds. To do so, he planted six seeds from the same plant in different flowerpots and exposed each one to different conditions. The scientist recorded the data in a table like the one below. Analyze

Flowerpot	1	2	3	4	5	6
Average temperature (°C)	0	5	10	15	20	25
Results after two weeks				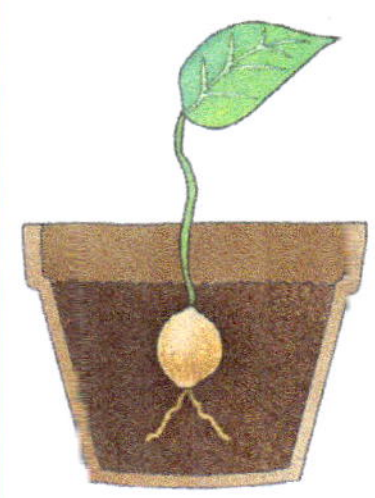		

a. What is the best temperature for the germination of this type of seed?

☐ 5 °C ☐ 10 °C ☐ 20 °C

b. What elements should be present for germination to occur?

☐ water ☐ air ☐ correct temperature

c. Which seed **did not** germinate?

☐ 2 ☐ 4 ☐ 6

Remember!

° is read as "degrees" and C stands for Celsius.

Let's Summarize

Germination is the process in which a seed, in the right conditions, develops and grows into a plant.

Pollination

Let's Connect

1. Find a lily to dissect. First, you will need to take off the petals. Then draw what you see. Observe
   a. Where are the seeds?

Petals come in many colors in order to attract insects, which help pollination.

The **pistil** is the feminine part of the flower. It has **specialized** parts for reproduction.

The **stamen** is the masculine part of the flower. It produces pollen.

The **sepals** are the protective, lower part of a flower. They are usually green.

What are the functions of bees and the wind in plant reproduction? Discuss with a partner.

In order for plants to reproduce, it is necessary that pollen from the stamen reaches the pistil. This movement is known as **pollination**, and it is made possible by **pollinators** such as insects, hummingbirds and the wind.

Let's Practice

2. Below is one of the methods used to make a plant produce flowers of a different color. Analyze

The stamens of a flower of one color are cut off. The pistil is left intact.	Pollen from a white flower is extracted with a brush.	The pollen is then transferred to the pistil of the colored flower.

a. What stage of the life cycle of plants does this method simulate?

☐ germination ☐ fruit formation ☐ pollination

b. What does the brush represent? Explain.

____

____

Education through Values

It is important to respect all living things. We take care of flowers because they are necessary for plants to reproduce and they make the environment beautiful. What can you do to protect flowers?

Let's Summarize

Pollination is the way plants reproduce and requires the movement of pollen from the stamen to the pistil. Some pollinators are insects, hummingbirds and the wind.

Fruit Formation

Let's Connect

Look at how the seed grows and how fruit is formed.

1

After pollination occurs in the flower, the seeds start forming inside the ovary.

2

Fruit is formed inside the flower as the walls of the ovary start to grow.

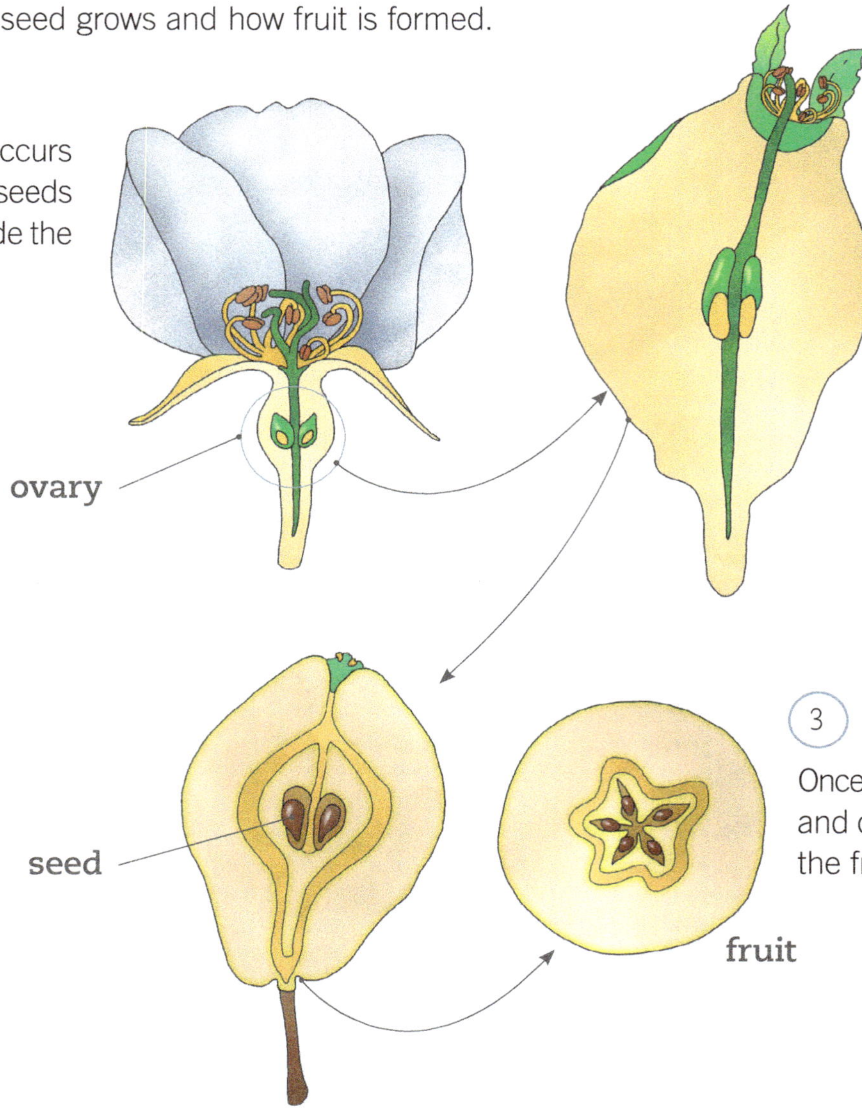

3

Once the walls of the ovary have grown and covered the seeds completely, the fruit is fully formed.

In order to make a new plant, seeds must get to a place where they can germinate and grow. This is known as seed **dispersal**. In order for seed dispersal to happen, dispersal agents are needed, including the wind and animals that eat fruit.

Staying Healthy

It is important to include fruits and vegetables in our diet. Experts recommend eating five portions a day.

Challenge

exhibit

Bring different fruits as a snack for a week and save the seeds. Then think of a creative way to display the seeds with a short description of what fruits they come from, which part of the fruit is the ovary and how the ovary protects the seed.

Let's Practice

1. Look at the pictures.

a. How does a flower turn into a fruit? Explain

Let's Summarize

After pollination, the seed starts to grow and is completely covered by the ovary until the fruit is formed.

Quiz Yourself

1. Describe the main stages of a flowering plant's life cycle.

Let's Check!

1. What do plants need to live? Mark with a ✔.

☐ water ☐ soil ☐ carbon dioxide

☐ oxygen ☐ shelter ☐ sunlight

2. Write the names of the main plant structures. Then match them with the parts in the picture.

☐

☐

☐

3. Complete the sentences.

The roots absorb ______________ and the ______________ that plants need to live.

The function of the stem is to ______________ water and nutrients.

Inside the ______________, ______________ occurs.

The ______________ process allows ______________ to make their own nutrients.

4. Match each concept in column A with its description in column B.

Column A	**Column B**
Pollination	It is inside the fruit and can make a new plant.
Flower	They are pollinators.
Fruit	This is the process where pollen is transferred from the stamen to the pistil.
Germination	This is the plant structure that comes from the flower and protects the seeds.
Seed	This is the plant structure where the reproductive organs are located.
Hummingbirds, wind, insects	This is the formation of a new plant from a seed.

5. How do bees contribute to plant reproduction? Explain.

____

____

How Did You Do?

For each ☺ color a ⬭.

The Importance of Plants

Plants and Animals

Let's Connect

1. Look at the pictures and answer the questions.

a. What do these animals' diets have in **common**? Compare

____

____

b. What other function can plants have for animals? Infer

☐ food ☐ protection ☐ shelter

nests: a structure in which a bird lays its eggs

Many animals use plants as **food**. For example, cows eat grass and pandas eat bamboo. Animals also use plants as **shelter**—in other words, as places that they can use for protection. For example, many birds build their nests in trees, and many insects live on stems, leaves or in tree trunks. Plants are important because they provide the **oxygen** animals need to breathe. It is very important to take care of plants, since they are necessary for the survival of all living things. One way to take care of them is to plant trees and create protected zones.

survival: continued existence

How can you take care of plants?

Let's Practice

2. Look at the picture. Grass is food for the rabbit, and the rabbit is food for the snake.

a. What would happen to the living things that eat plants if plants disappeared from the earth? Infer

____

____

b. What can you do to take care of grass? Propose

____

____

Let's Summarize

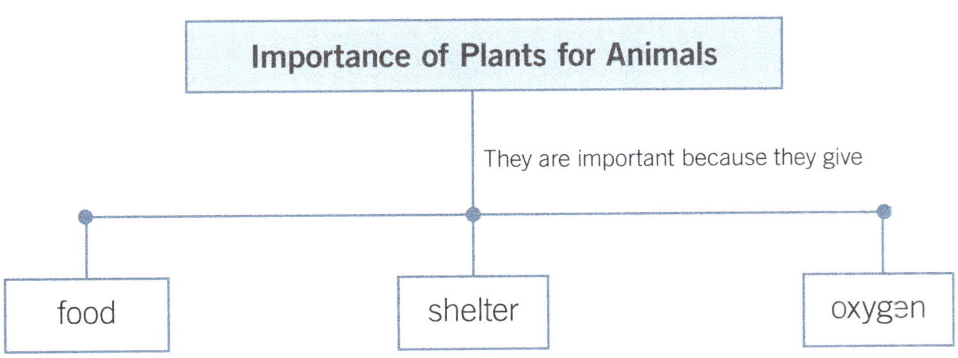

Plants in Our Lives

Let's Connect

Humans also benefit from plants. Some of their main uses are:

Food: Plants contain several nutrients, such as vitamins and minerals, that are very important to humans. For this reason, many plant parts are part of our daily diets.

Medicine: Many plants are used as home remedies—for example, chamomile and mint. Others are used in the pharmaceutical industry, such as willow bark, which is used to make aspirin.

bark: the covering of a tree trunk

Industry: Some plants provide us with useful materials, like wood or cotton, and allow us to make objects that we use daily.

Decoration: Because of their shape, color or smell, some plants are used to decorate, like orchids and carnations.

Talk with a partner about other ways we use plants.

Did You Know...?

Aloe vera is a plant that contains many beneficial substances for our bodies. More than seventy beneficial substances have been identified in aloe vera! For example, aloe vera helps heal scars and hydrate the skin, and it also disinfects.

scars: marks from an old cut

Let's Practice

1. Go to **Cutout 2** on **page 159** and classify the plants according to their uses. Classify

Food

Medicine

Industry

Decoration

Let's Summarize

Importance of Plants to Humans

- food
- industry
- medicine
- decoration

Plants and the Environment

Let's Connect

As you have already learned, plants have benefits for animals and humans. They are also important for the environment, mainly because photosynthesis produces oxygen, an essential gas for many living things.

Plants are also important for conserving soil because their roots protect it from **erosion**.

Plants are important for living things, so it is necessary to protect them and take care of them. To take care of plants, we should follow these recommendations:

mainly → principally

- Do not litter.
- Prevent forest fires.
- Do not cut flowers and branches.
- Do not remove bark from trees.
- Plant trees.
- Respect protected zones, such as national parks and reserves.
- Participate in reforestation campaigns.

litter → leave trash in public places

▲ Everglades, Florida

▲ Grand Canyon, Arizona

What other recommendations would you give to protect plants?

Let's Practice

1. How do plants help the environment? Explain

____

____

____

Let's Summarize

Plants are important for the environment because they supply oxygen and protect the soil from erosion.

Quiz Yourself

1. Why are plants important to animals?

____

____

____

2. How do humans benefit from plants?

____

____

____

3. Thinking about their importance to the environment, what measures would you recommend to take care of plants? Explain.

____

____

____

What Did You Learn?

1. Match each structure with its function.

Roots	Protects the seeds.
Leaves	Transports water to all the parts of the plant.
Flowers	Capture gases and sunlight and carry out photosynthesis.
Stem	Have the feminine and masculine reproductive organs.
Fruit	Absorb water and minerals.

2. Draw the life cycle of a flowering plant. Then explain the process.

3. Why are plants important to all living things? Explain.

4. Name five plants native to your country and propose ways of protecting them.

____

____

____

Scientific Skill: Infer and predict

5. Maggie bought a white carnation and put it in a clear vase of water. After a week, she noticed that there was less water in the vase than before.

a. Why does Maggie's vase have less water now?

____

____

____

b. If you put blue ink in the vase with the white carnation, what do you think would happen?

____

____

____

Collect a white carnation, a vase of water and some blue ink, and test your prediction.

How Did You Do?

For each ☺ color a ⬭.

Unit 2

Protecting Resources

Key Words

garbage

conserve

resource

organic

inorganic

In this unit you will learn to:

- distinguish and compare natural and artificial resources.
- classify waste according to material and decomposition time.
- explain the importance of using resources correctly and propose ways to reduce waste.
- build technological objects to reuse, reduce and recycle waste.
- formulate questions about objects and their surroundings.
- acknowledge and value the importance of water as a natural resource for the planet and all living things.

What Do You Know?

Initial Evaluation

1. Mark the situations where the environment is being protected with a ✔ and the situations where it is not with an ✖.

2. Why do you think the environment is not being protected in the situations marked with an ✖?

____

____

Scientific Skill: Formulate questions

3. Martha did the following experiment: First, she put some wet soil into two plastic containers. In one of the containers, she buried a plastic cap from a soft drink bottle, and in the other, she buried a piece of paper. She buried both items at the same depth. Then she left the containers in a place where they received sunlight and kept the soil wet for three weeks.

After three weeks, she checked the items and noticed that the plastic cap had not changed but the piece of paper had **deteriorated**.

buried: put under the ground

depth: distance below the surface

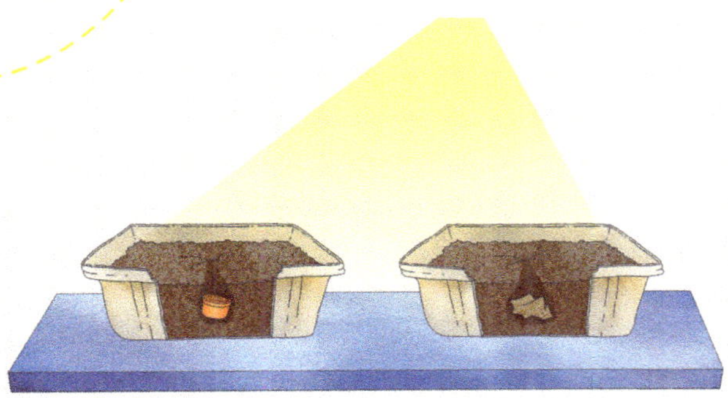

a. What should be the research question for this experiment?

☐ What will happen to a piece of paper and a plastic cap if left outside?

☐ Which material will **decompose** first?

Refer to the **Scientific Research Skills** foldout to recall what a **research question** is.

Do the same experiment as Martha and check her results!

Section 1

Types of Resources and Waste

Natural and Artificial Resources

Let's Explore

1. You will need the following materials for this activity: a nail, a sheet of paper and a piece of fabric. Look at them, touch them and then answer. Infer

a. What are these objects made of? Write the materials.

____

____

b. Where do the materials come from?

____

____

We use objects like pencils, books and fabrics daily. But have you ever asked yourself what these objects are made of or where they come from? Objects can be made of different materials, such as wool, plastic or metal. These materials come from **resources** available in the environment. Resources can be either **natural** or **artificial**.

fabrics: textiles

Natural Resources

Natural resources are raw materials that humans take from nature and use for their benefit. These resources can be **renewable** or **nonrenewable**.

Renewable Resources		Nonrenewable Resources	
These are resources that, after being used or extracted, have the capacity to regenerate—for example, trees, crops and animal resources. However, even though they can regenerate, if they are **overexploited**, they can be used up.		These resources **cannot** be renewed in a natural way after they have been used up, or if they can, it takes thousands of years to do so. We need to protect these resources so that they do not disappear. Some examples are coal, oil and mineral resources such as copper and iron.	 ▲ coal

used up: consumed to exhaustion

Artificial Resources

As we already know, our planet provides us with a lot of natural resources that we consume directly or use to make different products. However, all around us there are objects made of materials that do not come directly from nature but are **processed**. This means that these materials are created by humans from natural resources, and they are known as **artificial** or **man-made resources**.

These resources are used very often to make many objects we use daily, such as books, toys and bicycles.

objects for children to play with

Plastic is a flexible material whose **fabrication** requires oil. It is used to make toys, trash cans and some types of bags, among many other items.

Glass is mostly made from sand, plus other components in smaller quantities. It is used to make bottles, vases and windows.

grains on a beach

Ceramic objects are made out of a mixture of clay and other materials. Ceramic objects include cups, jars and porcelain.

Paper is made from wood pulp. Paper is used to make books, notebooks and napkins, among many other products.

paper to clean fingers while eating

Discuss with a classmate: what other man-made resources can you think of?

Types of Natural Resources

There are a large variety of natural resources. Some are renewable, like forestry, agricultural, livestock, fish and water resources, and others are nonrenewable, like mineral resources.

Mining resources are obtained directly from the ground. They include things like copper, gold, silver and iron.

Forestry resources are obtained from trees that are used for their wood.

Agricultural resources are resources from plants. Grains, fruits and vegetables are all examples of this type of resource.

Livestock resources come from animals. Some examples are milk, wool, leather and eggs.

Water resources are resources that come from water, either for consumption or to produce electricity.

Fishing resources come from water and are used for human consumption. Some examples are sardines, salmon, tuna and cod.

leather → animal skin used to make shoes, etc.

Did You Know...?

The Andes Mountain Range in South America has the biggest copper deposits on earth. Half the copper discovered on the planet comes from there.

Let's Practice

2. What are natural and artificial resources? Write down two examples of each. Define

Natural Resources	Definition	
	Examples	
Artificial Resources	Definition	
	Examples	

a. What is the difference between these two types of resources?

____

3. Name three renewable resources in your country. Identify

____

____

Let's Summarize

__________ resources can be found in nature and can be classified as __________ and __________.

__________ resources are __________ by humans with materials from nature.

Resources in my country include __________, __________ and __________.

Education through Values

Water is an **abundant** natural resource on earth, but only a small portion of it can be used by people. That is why it is so important to conserve it and keep it clean. What do you do to **preserve** this natural resource?

Waste

Let's Connect

1. Look at the pictures.

a. What does your family do with leftover food and empty containers? Identify

____

b. What other types of waste do you throw in the trash? Name

____

c. Where do you think this waste goes? Infer

____

Human beings use resources to make objects, but this process also produces a lot of **waste** or **garbage**. Waste is all the leftover material that cannot be used to make new objects.

Waste is normally put in places that are specially made to store it, such as **landfills** or **dumps**.

▲ garbage dump

Staying Healthy

In some homes, garbage or trash may accumulate and cause infection and disease. It is important to keep garbage in closed containers far away from the kitchen and other places where food is stored.

Classifying Waste

2. Look at the garbage can.

a. What kinds of things are inside? Infer

____

____

____

b. Can you classify this waste? Discuss

As you can see, there are different types of waste in the garbage can.

- Waste can be classified according to its **origin** and **composition**:

Organic waste is the leftovers of living things, such as leaves, fruit and vegetable peels, branches and food.	**Inorganic waste** is the leftovers of man-made materials. Some examples are plastic, **synthetic** fabrics and glass.

- Waste can also be classified according to the time it takes for it to **decompose**:

Biodegradable materials decompose naturally in a short amount of time. For example, a banana peel takes between two and ten days to decompose and paper between two and five months.	**Nonbiodegradable** materials take a long time to decompose. For example, it takes glass around 4,000 years to decompose and a plastic bag around 150 years.
quantity 	

Let's Practice

3. What is waste? Define

____

____

4. Go to **Cutout 3** on **page 161**. Glue the objects in the correct boxes. Classify

Organic waste	Inorganic waste

Did You Know...?

Some organic waste, like fruit peel and vegetables, can be composted. This process speeds up their decomposition with the help of microorganisms, worms and other living things.

speeds up → makes faster

Let's Summarize

Waste is all the leftover ____.

Waste can be classified according to its ______________________ as

______________________ or ______________________.

It can also be classified according to the time it takes to ______________________ as

______________________ or ______________________.

Quiz Yourself

1. Draw one natural and one artificial resource.

Natural Resource	Artificial Resource

2. What are the differences and similarities between the resources you drew? List them here.

Similarities	Differences
______	______
______	______

3. Match the types of waste with the correct containers.

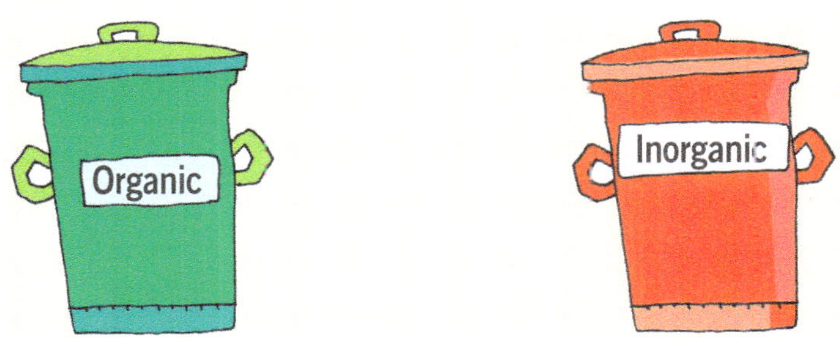

pear peel | can of tuna fish | rain boots | plastic bags | newspaper | wooden skewer

a. Which items are biodegradable?

______

b. Which are **not** biodegradable?

______

Let's Check!

1. Look at the pictures and identify if they show renewable or nonrenewable natural resources.

oil

aluminum

forests

water

______ ______ ______ ______

2. What do wool and wood have in common? How are they different? Mark with a ✔.

	Characteristic		
	Only wood	Shared	Only wool
Natural Resource			
Plant Resource			
Animal Resource			
Renewable Resource			

3. Write **T** for true or **F** for false. If the statement is false, explain why.

a. ______ Resources are used by humans to make objects.

____

b. ______ Artificial resources are made out of processed natural resources.

____

c. ______ Natural resources can be classified as renewable and nonrenewable.

____

d. ______ Plastic and paper are good examples of renewable natural resources.

____

4. Define **waste** and give three examples.

Definition: ____

____

____

Examples: ____

____

____

5. Look at the pictures. Classify the waste by writing it in the corresponding column.

Organic Waste	Inorganic Waste

How Did You Do?

For each ☺ color a ⬭.

Section
2 Protection of Resources

Appropriate Use of Resources

Let's Connect

1. Look at the picture.

a. Circle the natural resources in the picture. Identify

b. How are these people using the resources? Discuss with a classmate. Infer

c. How are these people protecting these resources? Discuss with a classmate. Explain

Our planet provides us with resources such as minerals, water, plants and animals. We constantly use these resources to feed ourselves, dress ourselves or build our houses.

Both renewable and nonrenewable resources can run out if they are **misused**. That is why we have to **protect them**, **use them responsibly** and **avoid actions that put their existence at risk**.

Some ways resources can be damaged are:

- deforestation
- water pollution
- accumulation of waste or garbage

feed → provide with food

Challenge

Humans have always used natural resources for daily life. Collect sheets of different colored paper and scissors. Cut each paper into ten 2-cm strips. Weave them together to make a place mat. Then glue the ends together and decorate it.

Measures to Protect Resources

You already know that resources can run out, but what can you do to help preserve them? Some **measures** that will help you protect essential resources are:

Do not leave the water running while you brush your teeth.

Turn off the lights when you are not in the room or do not need them on.

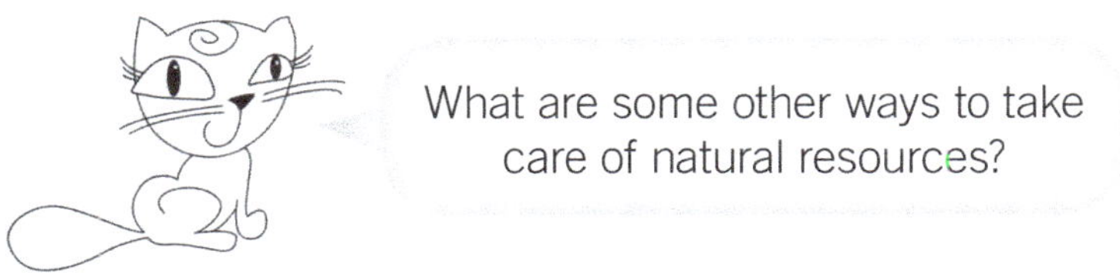

Plant trees and take care of plants.

Let's Practice

2. Which picture shows an appropriate use of resources? Identify

Let's Summarize

________________ natural resources can run out. Therefore, it is important to ________________ them, ________________ them responsibly and avoid actions that can put them at ________________.

Reduce, Reuse and Recycle

Let's Connect

1. Answer the following questions:

   a. What would happen if we filled the planet with garbage? Predict

   ____

   ____

   b. What recyclable materials are often thrown away? What objects can be made with them? Explain. Infer

   ____

   ____

Recycling Waste

Every day around one kilogram of recyclable material is thrown away per person. If you think of the number of people that live around you, the amount of waste produced in a day or a year is huge. But what can be done to lower the amount of waste? One option is to **recycle**. **Recycling** is the process of converting a used material into a new material. With these new materials, new objects can be made.

Arrow 1: Waste is collected.

Arrow 2: Recyclable material is processed and turned into new objects.

Arrow 3: People buy products made of recycled materials.

Go to **Activity Card 2** and learn how to recycle paper.

Recyclable Materials

Recycling protects the environment because it allows new objects to be made from materials obtained from waste. But is all waste recyclable? Unfortunately, not all materials are recyclable—for example, photo paper, mirrors, paint cans and some plastics cannot be recycled.

That is why it is necessary to separate recyclable materials into special containers. Here are some examples of different types of collection containers and some of the items that can be deposited there:

Plastic • bags • bottles **Aluminum** • food cans • soda cans	**Cardboard** • boxes • trays **Paper products** • newspapers • magazines	**Glass** • bottles • jars	**Hazardous Waste** • batteries • aerosol cans (anything considered dangerous)	**Organic or Biodegradable** • fruit and vegetable peels • food leftovers

Education through Values

Between 10 and 15 trees are needed to make 1,000 kilograms of paper. That is why every time you finish using your notebooks, you should remove the pages and dispose of them in a recycling container. You will be helping take care of the planet! What other materials can you recycle at home?

Reusing Waste

2. What can you make with a plastic bottle? Invent

____

____

3. Collect a 5-liter plastic bottle, scissors, soil and three seeds, such as lentils or beans. Ask an adult to cut the bottle in half. Then put some soil in both halves and bury the seeds. Water the seeds every two days. Draw what you made. Construct

a. How is the bottle being used now? What is its function? Infer

____

____

____

____

As we have already seen, it is very important to take care of the earth's natural resources. Another way of doing that is by **reusing products**. Reusing products lowers the amount of waste because they are used as many times as possible, less garbage is produced and fewer resources are used to make new objects. Some objects that can be used again are plastic bottles and tires.

Plastic Bottle	Tires

Reducing Waste

4. What can you do to produce less waste? Look at the picture and explain what you would do in this situation. Decide

a. What else could you do to reduce waste? Explain

There are some simple actions that people can do to **reduce** waste. Reducing means to decrease the number of unnecessary products that we use.

Some Ways to Reduce Waste

You should:

– buy products with less packaging.

– mend clothing. repair

– repair electrical appliances.

– use rechargeable batteries.

– reuse bottles once they are empty.

– use paper or fabric bags when you go shopping.

– not print on or use more paper than necessary.

Fun Fact!

There are companies that make plastic forks, knives, spoons and other items from corn. This means they are fully biodegradable and compostable. When you buy packaged goods or use bags, look out for these products!

Let's Practice

5. Make a toy, tool or utensil with reusable materials. Utensils such as penholders help us solve everyday problems. Construct

Before you make your toy, tool or utensil, think of something that you need. Write it down.

____

Then choose the reusable materials that you can use to make your object. Write the materials down.

____

____

Now design your object. Draw it.

What steps do you have to follow to make your object?

____

____

What is the function of your object? Explain it to a classmate.

Let's Summarize

Recycling is: ____.

Reusing is: ____.

Reducing is: ____.

Quiz Yourself

1. Why is it important to use the resources of our planet carefully?

2. Draw three types of waste that you find in your house.

Item 1	Item 2	Item 3

3. What can you do to reduce waste? Propose an action to reduce the waste in the previous activity.
   - Item 1
   - Item 2
   - Item 3

What is the Difference between Organic and Inorganic Waste?

Basic Framework

Thousands of kilograms of trash are produced on our planet daily. This waste can be classified as organic or inorganic according to where it comes from.

Observation

Look and answer.

What happened to the banana peel?

____

____

Where there any changes in the plastic cap?

____

____

Research Question

1. Which research question best fits your observations?

- [ ] Which type of waste takes less time to decompose?
- [ ] What do inorganic and organic waste have in common?

To create a research question, you need to **formulate questions** that will allow you to understand facts through experimentation. This type of question will lead to new questions to continue your research.

Hypothesis

Organic waste takes less time to decompose than inorganic waste.

Prediction

1. Mark what you think is going to happen if you put an apple peel and a plastic bag in a container outside.

- [ ] The plastic bag will decompose faster than the apple peel.
- [ ] The plastic bag will not decompose and the apple peel will.

Experimental Procedure

Supplies

– apple peel

– plastic bag

– two labeled containers, one with a label that says OW for organic waste, and the other IW for inorganic waste.

Steps

1. Put the peels in the OW container.
2. Put the plastic bag in the IW container.
3. Leave the containers outside for ten days.

   Write down the changes in both containers every two days.

Results

1. Complete the table.

Observations	Day 2	Day 4	Day 6	Day 8	Day 10
Apple peel					
Plastic bag					

2. Which object changes? Mark. ☐ apple peel ☐ plastic bag

Conclusions

1. Which waste is organic? ______________________
2. Which waste is inorganic? ______________________
3. Which type of waste takes less time to decompose? ______________________
4. According to the results, what is the difference between organic and inorganic waste?

____

In this experiment, you **formulated a research question** to prove a fact by means of experimentation.

What Did You Learn?

1. Write the names of three natural resources and three artificial resources in the table.

Natural Resources	Artificial Resources

2. Complete the diagram.

- Waste
  - origin or composition
    - ______
    - inorganic
  - ______
    - biodegradable
    - ______

3. Which situations contribute to the **preservation** of resources? Mark.

reforestation

pollution

recycling

Final Evaluation

4. Write an example of:

a. Recycling: ____________________

b. Reusing: ____________________

c. Reducing: ____________________

Scientific Skill: Formulate questions

5. Tom's teacher did an experiment in class. She used the following materials: a piece of thick plastic and a burner. She took the piece of plastic and held it in the burner's flame for a few seconds. Then she turned off the burner. **Warning**: this is an activity that only adults should do.

a. What do you think the plastic looked like after the experiment? Draw it.

Before putting it in the flame	After putting it in the flame

b. Which research question would you choose for this experiment?

☐ Is plastic a type of organic waste?

☐ What happens if you heat up a piece of plastic?

How Did You Do?

Find Test 2 Study Page

For each ☺ color a ⬭.

Unit 3

Food

Key Words

illness

healthy

unhealthy

hygiene

diet

In this unit you will learn to:

- classify foods by their effects on your health and propose healthy eating habits.
- propose, communicate and practice good hygiene to prevent illness while preparing food.
- observe, measure and record using scientific instruments and standardized units.
- recognize the importance of a balanced diet.

What Do You Know?

Initial Evaluation

1. Look at the images and circle using the key.
   healthy foods
   unhealthy foods

2. What other healthy foods can you think of? Name five.

3. Mark the environment where it is safe to eat lunch with a ✓.

4. Why do you think you should eat only in clean places?

medical revision

Scientific Skill: Use instruments to measure

5. Renee went to the doctor to get a checkup. The doctor **measured** and **weighed** her.

   a. What medical instrument did the doctor use to weigh Renee? Mark the correct picture.

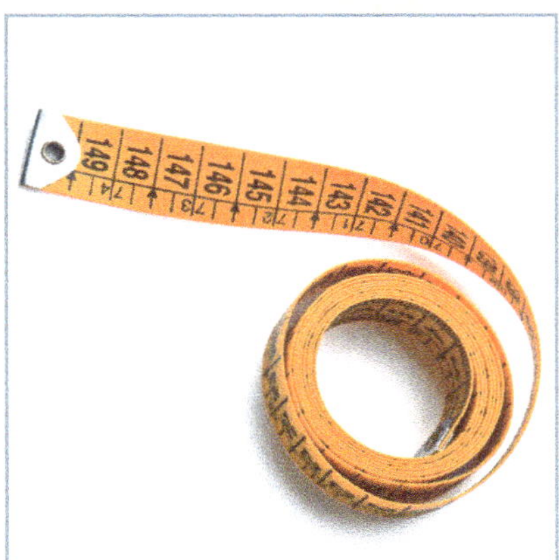

○ measuring tape

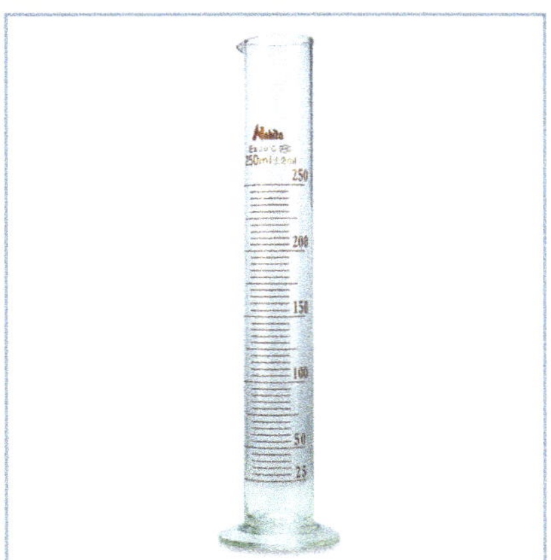

○ cylinder

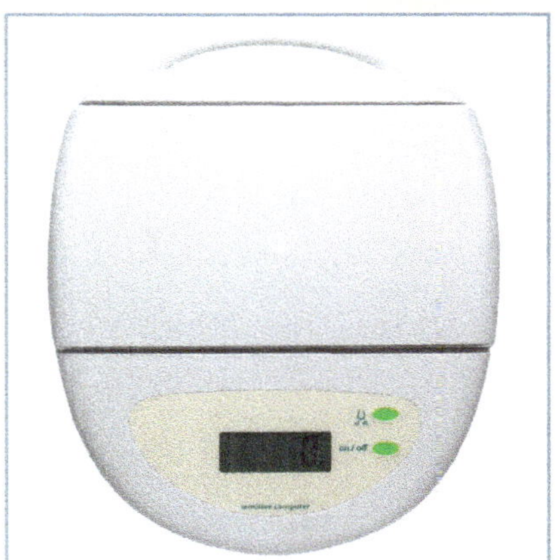

○ scale

   b. What unit of measurement is used to measure height?

☐ grams ☐ kilometers ☐ milligrams ☐ centimeters

Section 1

A Healthy Diet

Why We Need Food

Let's Connect

1. Look at the picture and answer the questions in your notebook. Identify

a. What do you eat for breakfast?

b. What do you recommend people eat for breakfast?

Nutrients in food provide your body with the necessary energy to do daily activities. In order to walk, study or play, you need to eat food. Food can be classified according to its origin, composition and function.

The **origin** can be a plant, as with grains, fruits and vegetables, or an **animal**, as with milk, eggs and meat.

Foods can be classified by their **composition** and **function**:

- those that have a lot of vitamins and minerals that help your body grow and function, like vegetables and fruits.
- those that have a lot of carbohydrates and give your body energy, like bread and cereal.
- those that help your body grow and heal because they have protein, like meat, eggs and milk.

Challenge

Do you think all people eat the same thing for breakfast? Do people from different countries eat the same things?

Let's Practice

2. Mark the foods that have an animal origin in and those that have a plant origin in . Identify

3. Complete the table with the foods listed below. Classify

lettuce | tomatoes | noodles | apples | meat | fish | bread | oatmeal | almonds

Types of Food		
Rich in Vitamins	Give You Energy	Help You Grow

Let's Summarize

In order to do daily activities, you need the energy obtained by eating ______________.

It is made of substances called ______________.

Food can have a ______________ origin or an ______________ origin.

Food can also be classified according to its ______________ and ______________.

A Balanced Diet

Let's Connect

1. Look at the picture and complete the activities. Identify

a. In the picture, mark the foods that are rich in vitamins.

b. Circle the child that is eating a healthy meal.

c. Which child do you think has a balanced diet? Why?

____

Could you only eat meat and drink milk every day? Definitely not! A balanced diet consists of a variety of foods that give you the necessary amounts of different nutrients. Children do not need the same amount or types of nutrients as adults because people's needs depend on age, weight, height and physical activity.

The **food pyramid** was created to display the amount of each type of food a person should eat daily. It is a chart shaped like a pyramid that shows you what you should eat more or less of. The foods at the bottom should be eaten in larger quantities, and the foods at the top in smaller quantities.

Staying Healthy

Do not forget to drink five or six glasses of water every day. Water is considered a nutrient because it is necessary for our bodies to function.

Let's Practice

2. Complete the following activities using **Activity Card 3**.

a. Circle the foods you should eat less of in red and those you should eat more of in green. Then name three foods you should eat more of and three you should eat less of. Identify

b. Create a menu based on a balanced diet for each day of the week including breakfast, lunch and dinner. Use the foods in the pyramid for your menu. Organize

3. Look at the table and answer the questions. Analyze

Age	23	65	10
Weight (kg)	56	78	40
Height (cm)	165	170	148
Physical Activity	2 times a week	2 times a week	4 times a week

a. Who does the most physical activity?

____

b. Who needs to eat more foods for growth and energy?

____

____

Let's Summarize

If you eat a variety of ____________________ that gives you the necessary nutrients for your body, you have a balanced ____________________.

The food pyramid helps us plan how much food we should eat ________________________________.

Healthy and Unhealthy Eating Habits

Let's Connect

1. Read the situation and answer. Apply

Your classmate always brings candy, chocolate-chip cookies, potato chips and a soda for lunch. What advice would you give about your classmate's eating habits?

a. Eat more:

☐ cookies and chips ☐ fruit and vegetables

b. Eat foods like:

☐ salad and nuts ☐ hamburgers and french fries

c. Always drink:

☐ eight glasses of water a day ☐ eight glasses of water a week

As you probably know, many people like to eat hamburgers, pizza and ice cream. However, these types of foods are high in **fat**, salt and sugar and can be harmful to your body if you eat them too often because they are **unhealthy**.

On the other hand, eating fruits, vegetables, grains and low-fat meats, milk and yogurt as part of your balanced diet are beneficial for your body because they are **healthy foods**.

Did You Know...?

Honey is considered a healthy food because it has nutrients that are necessary for your body, like sugar. It also has medicinal properties because it is an anti-inflammatory and a disinfectant.

Word Focus

Fat is a substance of animal or vegetable origin that is necessary for our bodies but is harmful if eaten in large quantities.

Education through Values

Cultural diversity is expressed in people's customs and traditions—for example, in the food they eat. It is important to respect the food preferences and customs of your classmates and family members.

Let's Practice

2. Read the text and answer the questions. Apply

Martina never eats breakfast before going to school because she would rather eat chips, french fries or ice cream. For lunch, she always has a salami sandwich, french fries with mayonnaise and ketchup, and a soft drink.

What kind of food does Martina eat? Mark with a ✔.

☐ healthy ☐ unhealthy

a. Suggest two healthy foods Martina could eat for breakfast and two for lunch.

____

____

3. A friend asks you to explain what healthy foods are. What should you say? Draw and explain your answer. Explain

Healthy Foods

____

____

Let's Summarize

Eating a ____________________ helps keep your body healthy.

Healthy Eating Habits

Let's Connect

1. Look at the picture and answer. Think about what you have learned and what you already know. Infer

a. Do you think it is healthy to eat in front of the computer? Why or why not?

____

____

b. How could the child's health be affected if he consumes only chocolate, potato chips and soft drinks?

____

____

Having **healthy eating habits** does not just mean having a balanced diet but also considering other aspects like:

- the amount of food you eat daily—for example, eat the portions appropriate for your age, height and physical activity. Also, remember that it is not good to eat late at night.
- the way you eat—for example, chew your food well, eat sitting up and not lying down, and do not eat too fast.
- good hygiene—for example, wash your hands before eating, brush your teeth after eating, and keep food and cooking areas clean.

Tip

Games like soccer, basketball and tag are all fun ways to do physical activity.

Did You Know...?

Obesity is a disease caused by eating too much unhealthy food and not exercising. People who have these bad habits develop too much body fat. This disease can cause other diseases or problems, like heart disease.

Let's Practice

2. Mark the healthy habits with a ✔. Identify

- [ ] Eating lying down.
- [ ] Washing your hands before eating.
- [ ] Eating in front of the computer late at night.

a. Do you have any of these eating habits?

____

____

Let's Summarize

Having healthy eating habits means having a balanced ______________, eating the correct ______________ for your body, thinking about the ______________ you eat and having good ______________.

Quiz Yourself

1. Place each food in the corresponding box.

ice cream	cookies
mayonnaise	candy
broccoli	hot dogs
melon	chicken
apples	kiwi

Healthy Foods	Unhealthy Foods

2. Suggest two healthy eating habits to a classmate.

- ____
- ____

Let's Check!

1. Complete the table by marking the origins of the foods with a ✔.

	Origin	
Food	**Animal**	**Plant**
Milk		
Asparagus		
Eggs		
Honey		

2. Go to **Cutout 4** on **page 161**. Glue the foods in the correct boxes.

Healthy Foods

Unhealthy Foods

3. Write **T** for true and **F** for false. If false, explain why.

a. ________ Foods that are high in fat are harmful to your health.

____

b. ________ To be healthy, you need to eat a balanced diet.

____

c. ________ People can suffer from diseases if they do not eat well.

____

d. ________ Nutrients only give your body energy.

____

e. ________ Fruits and vegetables give your body vitamins.

____

4. List three habits you could change in your diet to be healthier.

- ______________________________
- ______________________________
- ______________________________

How Did You Do?

For each color a .

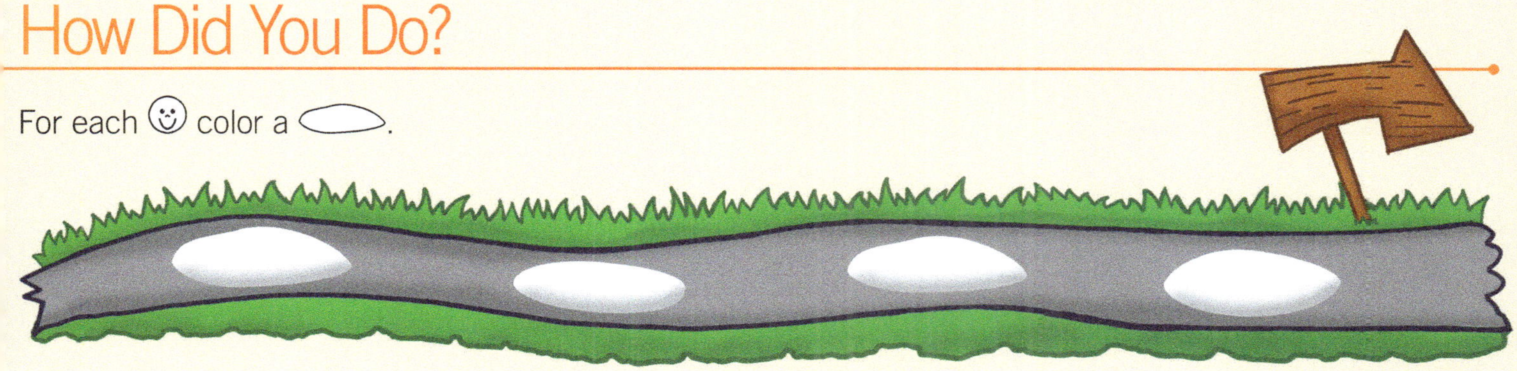

Handling Food

Clean and Fresh Food

Let's Connect

1. Look at the picture and answer.

situation 1

situation 2

a. In the second picture, circle nine differences between the two pictures. Compare and contrast

b. In which situation are the foods being handled and prepared properly? Explain

handled: manipulated with the hands

Before eating any food, it is necessary first to make sure it is clean and fresh (meaning it has not expired or become moldy). When you eat food that is moldy, has not been washed or has not been washed very well, microorganisms can enter your body and affect your health. In order to avoid this type of problem, it is necessary to have **good hygiene practices** when handling food.

Staying Healthy

October 15 is Global Handwashing Day. This simple action prevents **infections** and passing **contagious** diseases to others.

Word Focus

Microorganisms are small organisms that cannot be seen with the naked eye.

Let's Practice

2. Which of these practices could prevent food-related illnesses? Circle. Identify

3. Mark the practices that keep food clean with a ✓. Differentiate

- ☐ Cooking food well.
- ☐ Preparing food with clean hands.
- ☐ Washing your hands after going to the bathroom.
- ☐ Washing your hands before eating.
- ☐ Washing kitchen utensils very well.
- ☐ Having long, dirty fingernails.

fingernails: hard parts at the end of the fingers

Let's Summarize

Good Hygiene Practices

some examples are

The Importance of Washing Hands and Food

Let's Connect

1. Complete the table by writing what you think will happen. Predict

Situation	Behavior	What do you think will happen?
	Carla always washes fruit before eating it. If it falls on the ground, she washes it again.	
	Philip takes the food out of the refrigerator and eats it without washing it. If it falls on the ground, he picks it up and eats it anyway.	

Before you take food home, it has been handled by many people. Being touched by so many people is one of the reasons it can have harmful microorganisms that cause illnesses. Also, most foods, especially fruits and vegetables, have been treated with some sort of pesticide or other products that can affect your health.

To avoid infections or getting sick, follow these easy steps:
- always wash your hands with soap and water before eating.
- wash fruits well before eating them.
- wash vegetables under running water, and with some, like lettuce, make sure to throw away the outside leaves.
- before peeling fruits or vegetables, you also need to wash them.
- only use water, not soap or detergent, to wash fruits and vegetables.
- certain fruits, like strawberries, need to be washed more carefully because they grow close to the ground.

Word Focus

Pesticides are chemical substances used to protect plants from bugs or other animals that would eat them. Some pesticides are toxic to humans.

Let's Practice

2. Look at the situations. Apply

a. Draw a happy face next to the boy with good hygiene practices and a sad face next to the boy who could get sick.

b. How would you explain to the boy in the second situation that eating fruit without washing it could make him sick?

____

____

c. Write three ways the boy can prevent getting sick or getting an infection.

____

____

____

Let's Summarize

In order to stay ________________, it is important to ________________ the foods you eat.

Always wash your ________________ before handling food.

Choosing Packaged Foods

Let's Connect

1. Look at the picture and answer. Evaluate

a. Do you think what the girl said is correct? Why?

____

b. What did the girl see when she looked at the products?

____

c. What could happen if they eat food that has gone bad?

____

One important practice when buying food is to smell it and look at its color to make sure it is fresh. Also, make sure that cans are not **dented**, that the plastic covering the food does not have any holes and that the expiration date has not passed.

Did You Know...?

Before buying food, you should examine it to make sure it is fresh. For example, fresh fish should be firm and have shiny eyes and pink gills.

shiny → reflecting light

Let's Practice

2. Which foods would you buy? Go to **Cutout 5** on **page 163** and glue the pictures in the correct box. Identify

Foods You Would Buy	Foods You Would Not Buy

3. Look at the expiration date and the packaging date on a yogurt container. Analyze

a. What does each of these dates represent?

____

b. Why is it important to know this information?

____

____

Did You Know...?

Local authorities usually supervise the places where food is sold to make sure it is handled correctly and basic health standards are followed. This prevents the spread of contagious diseases among people.

Let's Summarize

Choosing Foods

canned food — without — ______

fresh food — that is not — ______

plastic-wrapped food — without — ______

Preventing the Spread of Illness

Let's Connect

If you eat foods that have not been washed properly or have gone bad, you could get illnesses like these:

Gastroenteritis

Most cases of gastroenteritis are caused by a virus, but with food it can be caused by bacteria. The inside of the stomach and intestine become inflamed, which causes vomiting, diarrhea and stomach pain.

Cholera

Cholera is an illness caused by eating food that has been contaminated by fecal matter. It causes stomach cramps, fever, nausea and diarrhea.

cramps: involuntary muscle contractions

Typhoid Fever

This illness is caused by eating food handled with dirty hands or contaminated by fecal matter. The symptoms are an intense headache, abdominal pain, red spots on the chest and constant fever.

spots: circular marks

Discuss with your classmates.

- Did you already know about these illnesses?
- What are their causes?
- What can you do to prevent them? Think of three ways.

In order to prevent these food-related illnesses, it is important to follow **food handling** standards. Things like keeping the kitchen clean, not **sneezing** on food, washing your hands before and after cooking, and keeping animals away from areas where food is prepared all help prevent illness.

sneezing: expelling air from the nose

Did You Know...?

Diarrhea is a symptom of an intestinal change in which water and minerals are lost in large quantities.

Word Focus

The **intestine** is part of the digestive system where nutrients are absorbed from food.

Let's Practice

1. How can you prevent illnesses caused by the incorrect handling of food? Differentiate

☐ Wash your hands before eating.

☐ Wash the kitchen table after using it.

☐ Eat fruits and vegetables without washing them.

Let's Summarize

To prevent illnesses like cholera and typhoid fever, follow basic food handling standards like:

- ______________________________
- ______________________________
- ______________________________

Quiz Yourself

1. List three basic practices of good food handling.

- ______________________________
- ______________________________
- ______________________________

2. Go to **Activity Card 4**. Draw one of the good hygiene practices. Then hang it up in your classroom.

3. At home, wash some lettuce with an adult. Then ask the adult if you did a good job. What did you do to get the lettuce clean? Write your answer here.

____

____

____

Vitamin C in Fruit

Basic Framework

Vitamins can be found in fruits and vegetables. A well-known vitamin is vitamin C. It helps us prevent colds and stay healthy. When some fruits are cut open, they change color, which means they have become oxidized. Vitamin C keeps fruits from oxidizing.

colds: mild viral infections of the nose and throat

Observation

Which foods would you eat to get vitamin C?

Research Question

How can we prove which fruits have vitamin C?

Hypothesis

If I add fruit juice that has vitamin C to a fruit that would normally become oxidized, the fruit will not change color.

Prediction

If I peel a banana, it will darken (change color). If I add fruit juice with vitamin C, it will not change color.

Experimental Procedure

Materials

- 4 vitamin C tablets
- 1 cup of apple juice
- 1 cup of orange juice
- 12 pieces of banana
- 4 plastic plates
- a graduated cylinder
- a bowl
- a spoon
- a scale
- distilled water
- a stirring rod
- a beaker

Steps

1. **Grind** the vitamin C in the bowl.
2. Measure 1 gram of vitamin C on the scale.
3. Put a piece of paper on the scale. Observe how the teacher returns the scale to zero.

4. Put the vitamin C on the paper and weigh it.
5. Measure 50 ml of distilled water into the cylinder.
6. Pour the distilled water and vitamin C into the beaker and mix it with the stirring rod.
7. Place three pieces of banana on each plate and label the plates 1–4.
8. Leave plate 1 as it is.
9. Add one spoonful of the vitamin C mixture to plate 2.
10. Wait five minutes. Observe and write what has happened to each plate in the **Results** section. Would the same thing happen if you added fruit juice to the bananas?
11. Now add orange juice to plate 3 and apple juice to plate 4.
12. Wait five minutes. Observe and write down your observations.

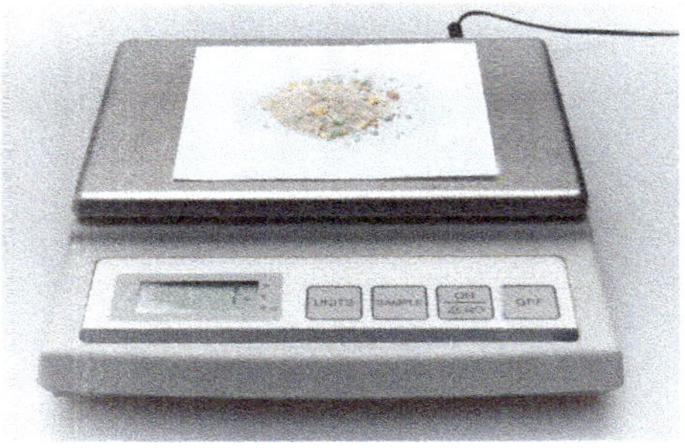

When you **work with scientific instruments**, you should always use them correctly, understand what they measure and follow safety guidelines.

To measure is to obtain precise information with the appropriate instruments.

Results

1. Explain what happened to the pieces of banana on each plate.

plate 1: ______

plate 2: ______

plate 3: ______

plate 4: ______

Conclusions

1. What instrument did you use to measure the weight of the vitamin C? ______
2. What did you use to measure the volume of the distilled water? ______
3. How can you prove which fruits have vitamin C?

______

What Did You Learn?

1. Classify the foods using the key.

plant origin   animal origin

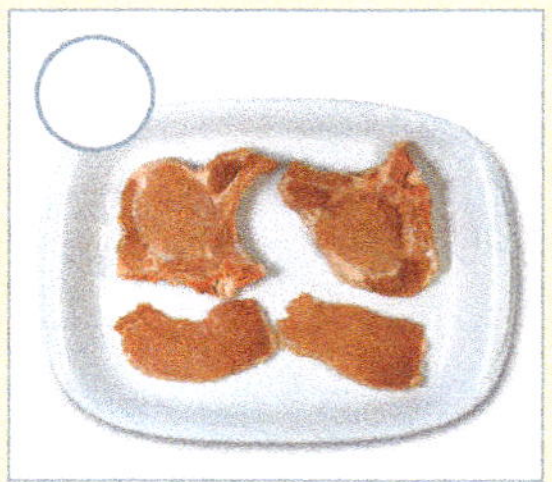

2. Name three healthy eating habits you can start today.

1: ______________________________

2: ______________________________

3: ______________________________

3. Create a poster to promote good food handling practices that prevent illness. The poster should have a title indicating the theme of the poster, a text about the theme and a drawing or photograph.

Scientific Skill: Use instruments to measure

4. Make delicious fruit juice in groups of three or four.

What Do We Need?

Oranges, bananas, water, a teaspoon of sugar, a scale, a 1-liter graduated cylinder, a pitcher, a blender and cups for everyone in the group.

What Do We Do?

- Wash your hands well, and make sure the area around you is clean.
- Use the scale to measure 500 grams of orange slices and 500 grams of banana (without the peel).
- Use the cylinder to measure 1 liter of water, and then add the water and fruit to the pitcher.
- Add sugar or honey. **Important**: take the pitcher to your teacher to **blend** the mixture in the blender.
- Pour the blended juice back into the pitcher. Use the cylinder to measure 250 milliliters for each member of the group.

a. What laboratory instruments did you use in this activity?

____

b. What units of measurement did you recognize from the activity?

____

How Did You Do?

For each ☺ color a ⬭.

Unit 4

Light and Sound

Key Words

vibrate

illuminate

ray

sound

light

In this unit you will learn to:

- distinguish between natural and artificial light sources.
- research through experimentation and explain certain characteristics of light.
- research through experimentation and explain certain characteristics of sound.
- summarize evidence from your observations to respond to a research question.
- value the importance of taking care of your hearing.

What Do You Know?

Initial Evaluation

1. In the drawing, mark the natural materials with a ✓ and the artificial materials with an ✗.

2. Why are windows made of glass and not metal? Mark with a ✓.

☐ To keep out water when it rains.

☐ To let light in so we can see through them.

3. Why are benches (a long seat for several people) made of wood and not glass?

____

Scientific Skill: Conclude

4. Look at the following pictures and answer.

▲ The girl can see through the window.

▲ The girl cannot see through the mirror.

a. What can you conclude from this situation? Mark your answer with a ✓.

☐ The girl can see through the window but not through the mirror.

☐ There are some objects that we can see through, like windows, and others that we cannot see through, like mirrors.

Section

1 Sources of Light

Luminous and Illuminated Bodies

Let's Connect

Have you ever observed what happens when day turns into night? When it becomes night, everything becomes dark and we cannot see objects clearly. On the other hand, during the day, the sun **illuminates** Earth and allows us to see everything around us.

Bodies that **emit,** or give off, light are called **luminous bodies**. The sun is the most important luminous body for our planet.

The sun, lightbulbs and stars are all examples of luminous bodies.

When the sun or another luminous body lights up an object, it allows us to see it. The objects or bodies that are lit by a luminous body are called **illuminated bodies**.

The table and your notebooks, pencils and backpack are all **illuminated bodies**.

Can you think of any other luminous bodies?

Word Focus

Body means the main physical part of a human or an animal, or an object that is separate from other objects, like planets in the solar system. How is the word used in the text?

Fun Fact!

The moon is a **satellite** of Earth that does not give off its own light. It shines because the sun illuminates it, so the moon is an illuminated body.

Let's Practice

1. Look at the picture.

a. Complete the table. Identify

Luminous Bodies	Illuminated Bodies

b. Why is the flashlight a luminous body? Explain

____

____

Let's Summarize

Bodies that give off light are ______________________________.

Bodies that are illuminated by others are ______________________________.

Luminous bodies light up illuminated bodies.

Natural and Artificial Light Sources

Let's Connect

Luminous bodies are sources of light, so they are also called **luminous sources** or **light sources**. There are two types of light sources: natural and artificial.

Natural light sources emit their own light and can be found in nature. Examples of these are the sun, stars and some insects like glowworms or fireflies.

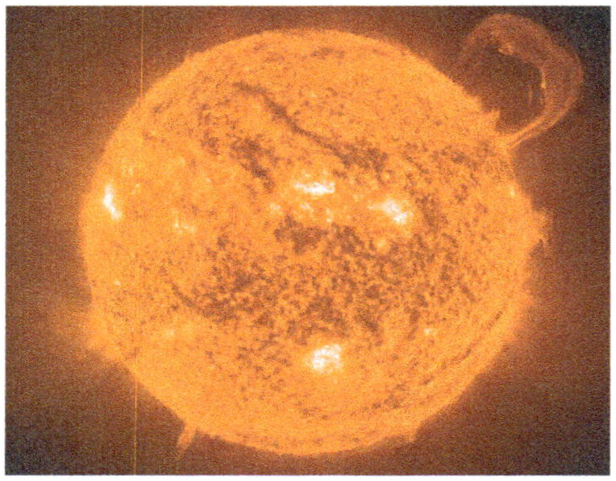

▲ the sun

▲ glowworm

Artificial light sources are made by humans and also emit light. Examples of these include when you turn on a lamp or light a candle or match.

▲ candle

▲ match

Education through Values

LED lights—used in flashlights, televisions and remote controls—are artificial light sources. They are more **efficient** than normal lightbulbs, and using them helps protect the environment because they consume less energy and last longer. If you choose to use this type of technology in your house, you will be respecting the environment.

persist

Let's Practice

1. Go to **Cutout 6** on **page 163**. Glue the light sources in the correct boxes. Identify

Natural Light Sources

Artificial Light Sources

Let's Summarize

Light sources can be ______________________________ or ______________________________.

Quiz Yourself

1. What are the differences between a luminous body and an illuminated body?

____

____

2. Complete the table with the characteristics of natural and artificial light sources.

Natural Light Sources	Artificial Light Sources

How Light Travels

Let's Explore

1. Look at the picture and answer the questions.

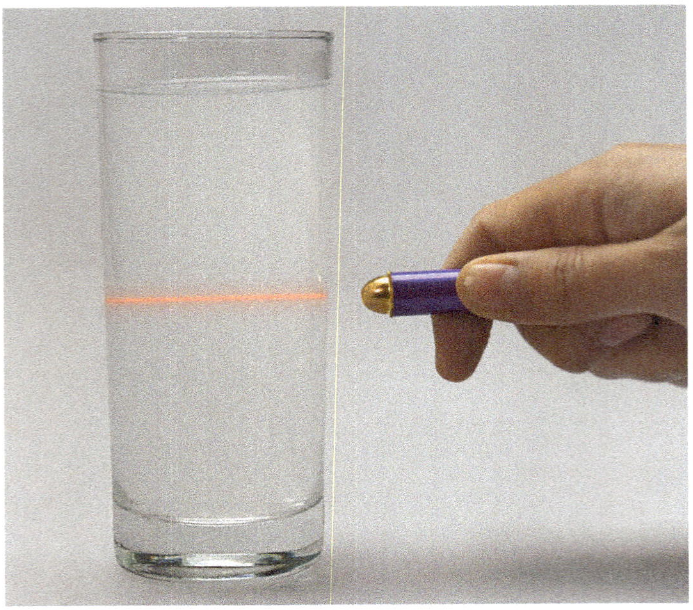

a. What happens when you point the light from the laser pen at the glass of water? Explain

____

____

____

b. Why do you think you can see the light inside the glass? Infer

____

____

____

The light shines through the glass in a straight line. This experiment shows one of the **properties of light**: light travels in a **straight line**.

2. Collect a shoe box and a pencil. Use the pencil to poke holes in different parts of the box. Then place a light inside of the box, as shown in the photograph. Experiment

a. What happens? Does light shine through all the holes or only some of them?

____

____

Light should shine through all the holes because the lightbulb emits light in all directions. This experiment shows that **light propagates** or **spreads in all directions**, which is another **property of light**.

To obtain better results, turn off the light and close the curtains.

Let's Practice

3. Look at the following picture and answer. Explain

a. What happens to the sunlight as it enters the room?

____

____

b. What property of light is seen in the picture?

____

____

c. What is another property of light?

____

____

Did You Know...?

The speed of light is 299,792,458 meters per second or 1,080 million kilometers per hour! Nothing travels faster than light. It is so fast that light from the sun, 150 million kilometers away, only takes eight minutes to reach Earth.

Let's Summarize

Some Properties of Light

are

Transparent, Translucent and Opaque Objects

Let's Explore

1. Collect a drinking glass, a piece of tissue paper and a piece of cardboard. Try looking through each material, as shown in the pictures below. Experiment

   a. What happens with each material? Discuss with your classmates.

Transparent objects are things we can see through easily because light passes through them completely. For example, a drinking glass and a window are transparent.

Translucent objects are things we can see through but not clearly. Light does not pass through them completely. An example of this is tissue paper.

Opaque objects are things we cannot see through. Light does not pass through them. An example of this is a piece of cardboard.

2. **Shine** a flashlight on any opaque object, as seen in the picture. Experiment

   a. What happens?

   ____

   ____

   ____

   ____

   ____

When an opaque object blocks the passage of light, it creates a dark area called a **shadow**.

Let's Practice

3. Describe the characteristics of each type of object. Describe

Transparent	
Translucent	
Opaque	

4. Mark the translucent object with a ✔ (red), the transparent object with a ✔ (green) and the opaque object with a ✔ (blue). Identify

pitcher

jacket

bottle

Let's Summarize

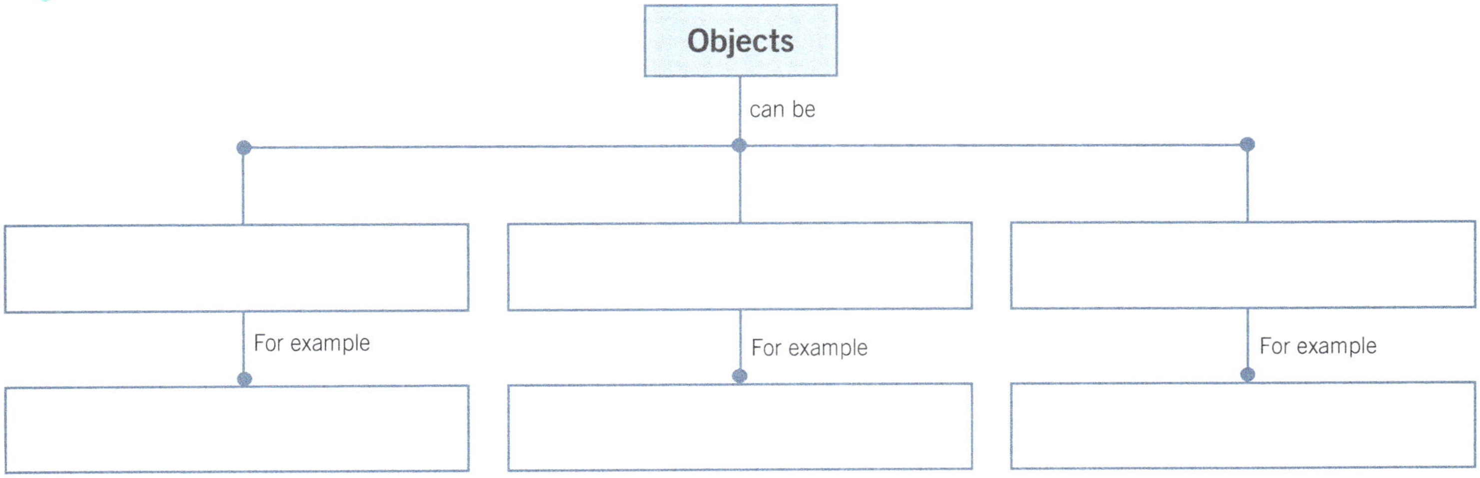

Reflection of Light

Let's Explore

1. For the following experiment, you need only a mirror. Observe

Place the mirror in front of you and observe.

a. What do you see?

____

____

When looking at the mirror, you can see your body because light reflects in the mirror.

The rays of light that reflect off your body travel in a straight line toward the mirror. When they hit the mirror, they reflect off it at exactly the same angle, which allows you to see yourself in the mirror.

Now, with a classmate, place the mirror on the wall. Each of you should move to one side so that the mirror is in the middle, as seen in the picture.

b. Can you see your classmate?

____

____

The picture shows that the light that reflects off your classmate's body hits the mirror and reflects toward you. This is why you can see each other. The ray that reaches the mirror is called the **incident ray**, and the ray that is reflected is called the **reflected ray**.

toward → in the direction of

Fun Fact!

Mirrors are actually just pieces of glass that have been painted with a special type of paint that reflects light. Some people believe that breaking them causes seven years of bad luck!

Challenge

farther → a greater distance

Do the previous activity again, but this time stand farther away from the mirror than your partner. Can you still see each other? Stand farther to the side; can you see your partner now? When can you not see your partner anymore? What do you think this means about the angles of reflected rays?

Let's Practice

2. Look at the image. It shows a light from a flashlight that is shined on a mirror.

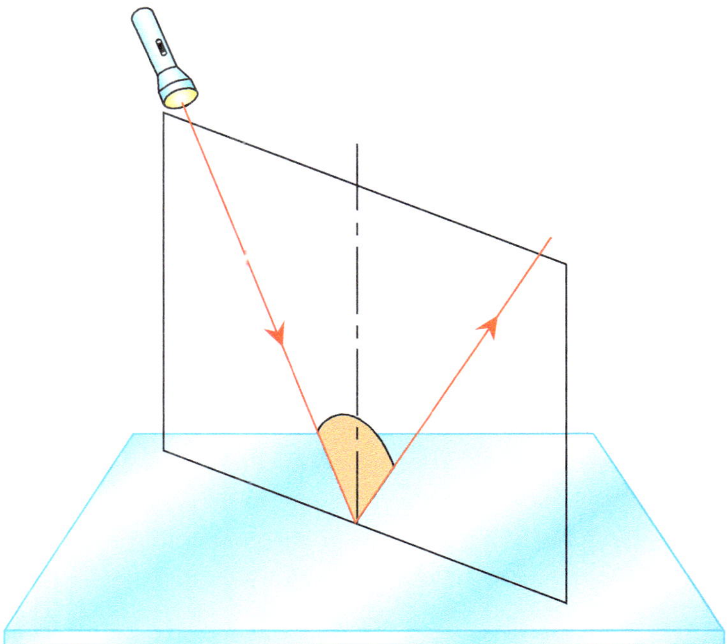

a. What happens? Explain. Explain

____

____

____

b. Which is the incident ray? Identify

____

____

____

c. Which is the reflected ray? Identify

____

____

d. What are the angles of the rays? Recognize

____

____

Let's Summarize

Light can ______________________, which is a phenomenon that consists of ______________________

____.

The ray that hits the mirror is called the ______________________.

The ray that is reflected from the mirror is called the ______________________.

Refraction of Light

Let's Explore

1. Collect a clear glass and a pencil. Fill the glass with water. Look at the pencil and observe its shape. Now put it in the cup and see what happens. Explore
   a. What difference can you see in the pencil after it was placed in the water?

   ____

   ____

   ____

   b. Why do we see the pencil as being bent? Infer

   ____

   ____

   ____

   ____

The water does not bend the pencil. Instead, the light changes direction slightly when it comes out of the water, making it look like the pencil is bent. (slightly → not much; bend → curve)

Light travels faster through air than through water. So when light enters the water, it slows down slightly and no longer travels in a straight line. That is why it looks like the pencil looks bent. This is called **refraction of light**.

Refraction of light occurs when a ray of light changes direction as it passes from one medium to another. An example of this is when light passes from air to water or oil to water.

Did You Know...?

The lenses of eyeglasses curve light so that the person who uses them can see better.

Word Focus

A **medium** is a condition or an environment.

Let's Practice

2. Complete the following experiment. You will need a coin and a cup.

Experiment

- Place the coin in the cup and while staying close, position yourself so that you cannot see the coin. Use the image as a reference.
- Slowly add water to the cup until you have filled it all the way.

The coin should not move, so make sure to pour the water slowly down the side of the cup.

a. What differences did you observe before and after adding water?

Before: ______________________________

____

After: ______________________________

____

b. What property of light did you observe during this experiment?

____

c. Why can you see the coin only when you add water? Explain.

____

____

Let's Summarize

Light can experience a phenomenon called ______________________, which means ______________________________.

Dispersion of Light

Let's Connect

1. Look at the image and answer.

a. Why do you think you can see several colors? Predict

____

____

____

White light consists of several colors. When light passes through a prism, the colors are separated, or dispersed. This group of colors is known as the **light spectrum**, and the phenomenon is known as **dispersion of light**.

Fun Fact!

The same thing happens when it rains and a rainbow forms. The sun shines through the drops of water, and then the light separates into all the colors you can see in the rainbow.

Word Focus

A **prism** is a transparent body with flat surfaces that are not parallel.

Let's Practice

2. To prove that white light consists of all the colors in the light spectrum, build a Newton disc. Go to **Activity Card 5** and follow the instructions. Prove

a. What happens when you spin the disc? rotate

____

b. Can you conclude that white light consists of all the colors on the disk? Explain.

____

Let's Summarize

During the phenomenon of light dispersion, white light ____

____.

Quiz Yourself

1. Identify the property of light related to each picture, and explain what happens.

____

____

____

____

____

____

____

____

____

____

____

____

Does Light Travel Only in a Straight Line?

Basic Framework

Light is emitted by light sources. Light travels in a straight line and propagates in all directions.

Observation

Look at the picture.

1. What do you see in the picture?

____

____

2. What shape are the sun's rays?

____

____

Research Question

Can light change direction if it passes through holes that are not **aligned**?

Hypothesis

The light will not change direction when passing through holes that are not aligned.

Prediction

If you shine a light through the hole in one piece of cardboard onto another piece of cardboard with a hole in a different place, what do you think will happen? Mark your prediction with a ✔.

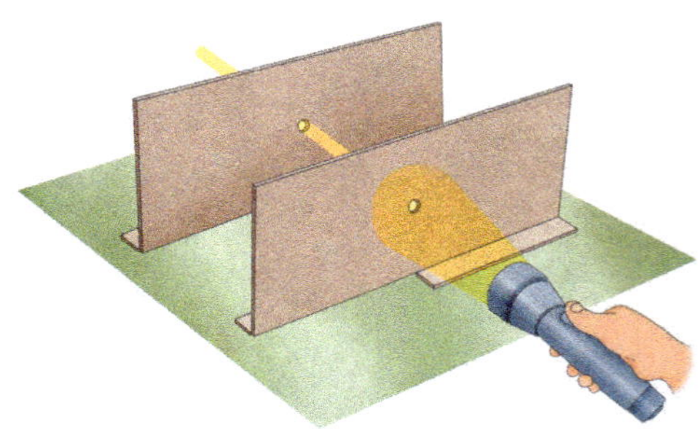

☐ The light will shine through the holes in both pieces of cardboard.

☐ The light will shine through the hole in the first piece of cardboard and spread in all directions when it hits the second.

Experimental Procedure

Supplies

Cardboard, scissors, a flashlight and a pencil.

Steps

1. Go to **Cutout 7** on **page 165** and cut out the template.
2. Copy the template three times on the cardboard.
3. Poke a hole in the cardboard with the pencil where indicated.
4. Set up the cardboard as shown in the picture.
5. Turn on the flashlight and ask a classmate to see if light is shining through the third hole.
6. Then move the middle piece of cardboard so that the holes are not lined up, and see if the light shines through the third hole.

Results

1. What happened to the light when the pieces of cardboard were aligned?

____

2. What happened to the light when the pieces of cardboard were not aligned?

____

3. When the cardboard pieces are not aligned, how does the light need to move to shine out of the third hole?

____

Conclusion

ray

1. Can a **beam** of light change direction when passing through holes that are not aligned? Explain.

____

____

To establish the **conclusion** to this experiment, you should analyze the results and use them to answer the research question.

Let's Check!

1. Circle the natural light sources in (red) and the artificial light sources in (blue).

2. Which of the following statements is **incorrect**? Mark it with an ✗.

   A. Light travels in a straight line.
   B. Light travels in a curved line.
   C. Light propagates in all directions.
   D. Light travels at different speeds in different mediums.

3. What is the difference between transparent and translucent objects? Explain.

____

____

4. What characteristic does an object have if it creates a shadow when light is shined on it? Explain.

____

____

5. Use a drawing to explain what happens in each phenomenon. Give examples.

The Reflection of Light

The Refraction of Light

The Dispersion of Light

How Did You Do?

For each color a .

Section 3

Sound

The Origin of Sound

Let's Explore

1. Find a guitar and pluck one of the strings so that it **vibrates**. Explore
   a. What happens?

   ____

   b. Make the string vibrate again, and then stop it. What happens?

   ____

When the string vibrates, it produces a sound. When it stops vibrating, the sound can no longer be heard. From this observation, you can **conclude** that **sound is produced from the vibration of an object.**

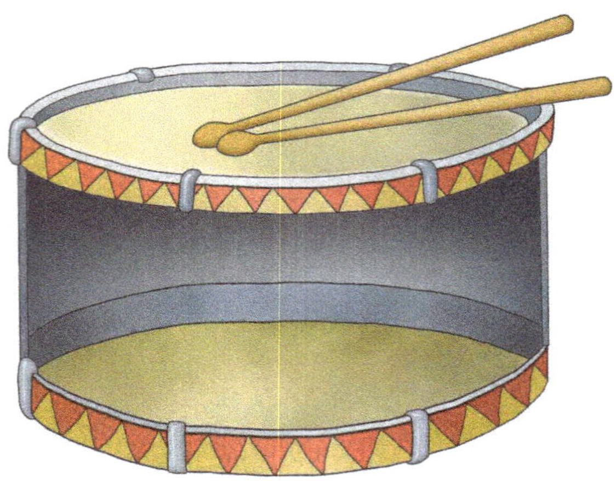

▲ When you pound on a drum with your hands or drum sticks, the air inside it vibrates and produces a sound.

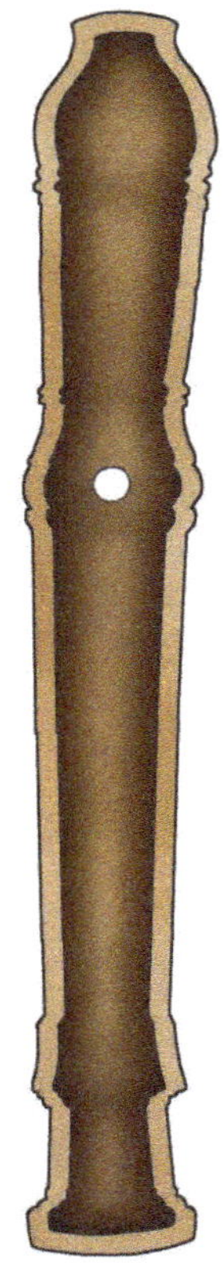

▲ When you play a recorder, the air passing through it vibrates and produces a sound.

When the bell rings at your school, do you always hear it? Discuss.

Sound can be heard from many different places near the source because sound **propagates in all directions**.

Let's Practice

2. Collect the following supplies: a toilet paper roll, a balloon, a small mirror, tape, scissors, glue and a flashlight. Experiment

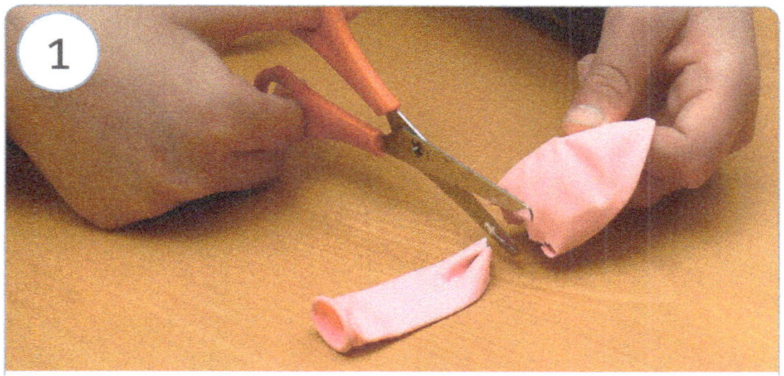

Cut off the end of the balloon.

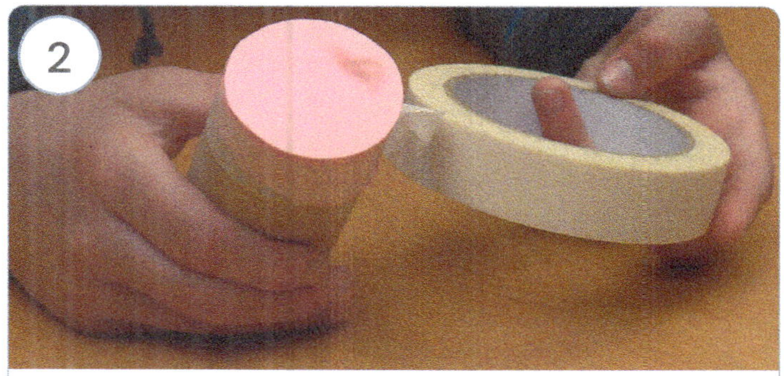

Tape the top part of the balloon over the toilet paper roll.

Glue the mirror on one side of the balloon (not in the middle).

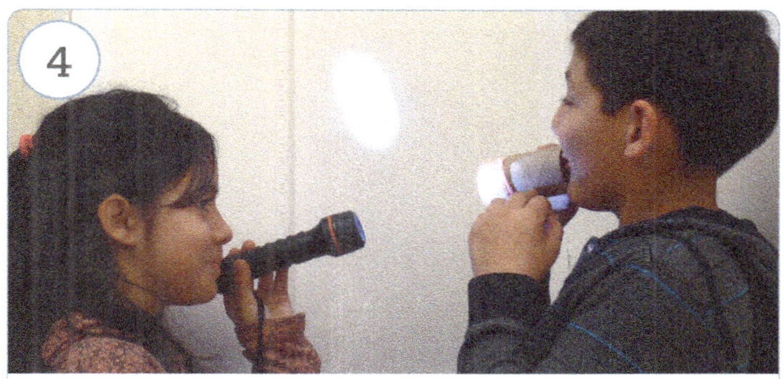

Point the roll at the wall and have a classmate shine a flashlight on the mirror. Now talk into the tube and observe what happens.

a. What happened to the mirror's reflection on the wall?

____

b. How can you explain these results?

____

Let's Summarize

Sound is produced by the ____________________ of an object. Sound propagates in all ____________________.

The Transmission of Sound

Let's Explore

1. Sound can be transmitted from one place to another. Let's see how it works. Collect two empty yogurt containers and two meters of yarn or string. Experiment

- With the help of an adult, poke a hole in the bottom of each yogurt container. Put the yarn through the hole in one yogurt container.
- Tie a knot in the yarn.
- Put the other end of the yarn through the hole in the other container and tie another knot.
- With a classmate, take one container each and move away from each other.
- Pull the containers apart until the string is taut. Then have one person talk into the container while the other puts an ear to the container and listens. Remember to always keep the string **taut**.

a. What happened when you did this activity? Could you hear your classmate talking?

____

____

____

When you speak into the yogurt container, it vibrates the air inside the container. This vibration of the air makes the yarn vibrate and carry the vibration to the other end. Then the yarn makes the air in the other yogurt container vibrate, allowing the other person to hear your voice.

Sound is transmitted from one place to another and through different mediums. These mediums can be liquids, like water; solids, like yarn; or gases, like air.

Tip

Cover your other ear to make sure you are only listening to the sounds coming from the container.

Word Focus

Taut means to be stretched or pulled tight.

Fun Fact!

We can hear sounds thanks to our ears. This organ perceives vibrations through the outer ear. The vibrations then pass along a duct to the eardrum, where they are transmitted to a fluid in the inner ear and converted into electrical signals that are sent to the brain.

Let's Practice

2. Look at the following picture. Apply

a. What produces the sound of the bell?

____

____

b. How does the sound of the bell get to our ears? Explain.

____

____

c. What medium does the sound use to travel to our ears?

____

Let's Summarize

Sound can ______________ through different mediums. These mediums can be ______________, ______________ or ______________.

Characteristics of Sound

Let's Connect

Sounds have different characteristics, like **intensity** and **tone**.

- **Intensity**

  Listen to the sounds in your classroom. Which sounds are louder and which are softer? **Sound intensity** allows us to classify sounds as **loud** or **soft**. For example, when someone **yells**, the sound is loud. On the other hand, when someone **whispers**, the sound is soft.

  The intensity of sound is measured with an instrument called a sound level meter, and the unit of measurement is a decibel. The table shows the intensities of certain sounds.

Intensity of Certain Sounds

Sound	Intensity (decibels)
A whisper	30
A normal conversation	50
A vacuum cleaner	70
Car horn	80
A siren	120
A plane taking off	150

- **Tone**

  Is your mom's voice the same as your dad's? Surely, they are different! Their voices sound different because of their tones: one is deeper (your dad's) and the other is more high-pitched (your mom's). **Tone** allows us to classify sounds as **deep** or **high-pitched** and relates to the physical property called **frequency**. Deep sounds have low frequency, and high-pitched sounds have high frequency. Frequency is measured in **hertz**.

  Humans can hear deep and high-pitched sounds between the frequencies of 16–20,000 hertz.

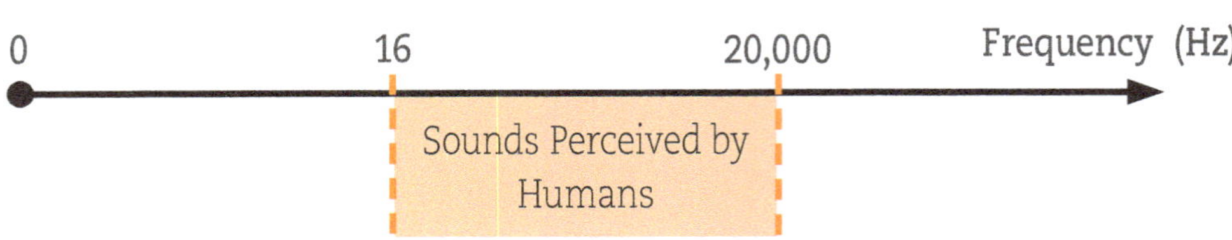

Did You Know...?

Dolphins make sounds that have frequencies between 2,000 and 100,000 hertz.

▲ whisper

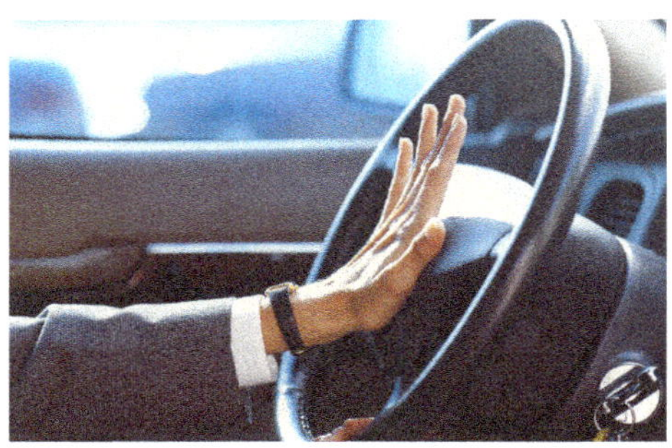

▲ car horn

▲ plane taking off

Let's Practice

1. Number the sounds in order of intensity from highest to lowest Apply

☐ A cat purring. ☐ A baby crying. ☐ A balloon popping.

2. Mark the animals or object that make a deep sound with a ✔. Apply

Staying Healthy

Do not expose yourself to sounds that hurt your ears because they can damage your sense of hearing. Be especially careful when you listen through headphones.

Let's Summarize

The Characteristics of Sound

are

- intensity
  - can be
    - loud
    - ______
- ______
  - can be
    - ______
    - high-pitched

The Absorption of Sound

Let's Explore

1. Collect a battery-powered radio and an insulated box big enough to fit the radio inside. Experiment

a. Turn on the radio. What happens?

___

___

___

b. Now put the radio in the box and close it. Can you still hear the radio?

___

___

___

What happens to the sound of the radio when it is inside the box? The sound **decreases in intensity** because the box **absorbs** part of the sound and reflects the other part. When a sound travels from one medium to another, part of the sound is absorbed. The same thing happens inside your house: sounds are absorbed by the furniture, rugs and curtains.

rugs → floor coverings

Let's Practice

2. Use a drawing to explain how sound would be absorbed by a foam wall. Describe

3. List two examples from daily life where sound is absorbed. Explain what happens to the sound intensity in each case. Apply

Example 1:

____

____

____

Example 2:

____

____

____

Let's Summarize

Sound decreases in intensity because ____.

The Reflection of Sound

Let's Connect

1. Look at the following situation.

a. What emits sound? Who receives sound? Identify

____

b. What happens to the sound waves when they hit the wall? Infer

____

The sound coming from the radio travels through the air in all directions and hits the wall. As we have seen, one part of the sound is absorbed by the wall and the other part is reflected and returned. When a sound is reflected, it **changes direction** and **loses energy**—in other words, it **loses its intensity**.

The **quantity of sound that a material reflects** depends on the material's characteristics. For example, concrete reflects sound very well; on the other hand, a curtain absorbs part of it and reflects the rest.

Do you know what produces an echo? When a sound is reflected and then travels back to the place where it started after a certain amount of time, it produces an **echo**. There are places where if a person shouts or talks, they hear their voice again a moment later, which means they are hearing their echo.

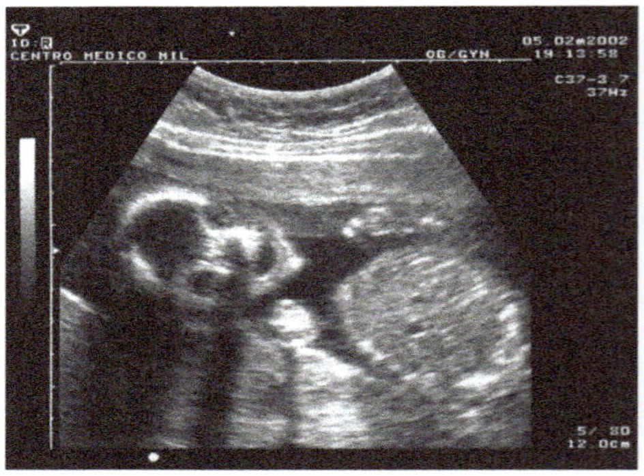

▲ Sound reflection has many uses—for example, in ultrasounds or sonograms. Ships also use sonar technology to navigate and to detect objects underwater.

Let's Practice

2. Use a daily situation to explain how sound is reflected. Use a drawing to help you explain. Describe

____

____

____

____

____

Let's Summarize

Sound reflection is a property in which sound changes ____________ and loses ____________.

The quantity of sound that a material reflects depends on the material's ____________.

Quiz Yourself

1. A girl put her alarm clock underneath her pillow to be able to hear it better in the morning. However, the alarm went off and she did not hear it. Think of this situation and answer.

a. Why did the girl not hear the alarm clock?

____

b. What phenomenon explains what happened?

____

c. What characteristic of sound decreased so that the girl did not hear the alarm?

____

d. Where should the girl put the alarm clock in order to hear it better?

____

What Did You Learn?

1. Write an **N** next to the natural light source and an **A** next to the artificial light source.

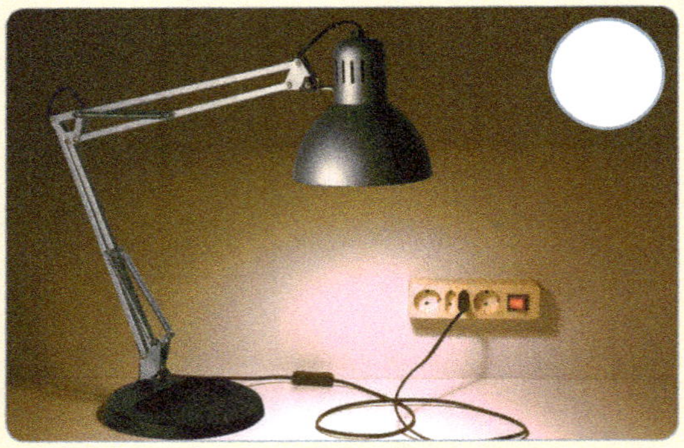

2. Look at the picture.

a. Draw the shape in which the rays of light travel toward the book.

b. Could the girl read the book with the lamp turned off? Why or why not?

3. Find a glass of water and a sheet of white paper. Place the glass of water on the paper in the sunlight, and observe the different colors on the paper. What phenomenon can explain what happened?

____

____

____

4. Which of these is a property of sound? Mark the correct answer with a ✔.

A. Sound only travels in a straight line.

B. Sound travels in a curved line.

C. Sound propagates in all directions.

D. Sound does not propagate.

Scientific Skill: Conclude

5. Claudia is in a room where a stereo is playing music very loudly. She then goes to the next room and the sound is less intense. Thinking about the characteristics and properties of sound, what can you conclude?

____

____

____

How Did You Do?

Find Test 4 Study Page

For each ☺ color a ⬭.

Unit 5

Earth and the Solar System

Key Words

universe

solar

lunar

axis

phase

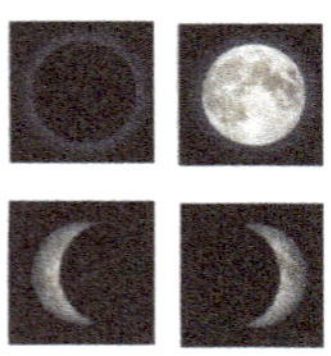

In this unit you will learn to:

- describe the characteristics of various components of the solar system.
- explain the rotation and orbital revolution of Earth.
- explain solar system events.
- construct models that simulate events in the solar system.
- communicate and compare observations about the phases of the moon using simulation.
- value the importance of working as a team.

What Do You Know?

Initial Evaluation

1. Write the time of day for each picture.
2. What differences do you see between the pictures? Explain.

____

____

3. How many hours make up one full day on Earth? _____ hours.
4. What are the names of the times of the day?

____

Scientific Skill: Communicate and compare

5. Does the sun **set** at a different time each day? To find out, use a watch and a notebook. Write down the time of the **sunset** for three days.

   a. Complete the table.

Day 1	Day 2	Day 3
_____ : _____	_____ : _____	_____ : _____

   b. Did the sun set at a different time each day? Mark with a ✔. ☐ yes ☐ no

   c. Compare your results with your classmates. Are they the same?

   ____

   d. Why do you think the sun sets at different times?

   ____

   ____

   ____

   e. With your class, come to a conclusion about what time the sun sets. Then write it on a poster and hang it up in the classroom.

Section 1 # The Solar System and Its Components

The Universe

Let's Connect

When was the universe formed? It is thought that the universe began to form about 14,000 million years ago as the result of a huge explosion called the **Big Bang**.

In order to understand the universe, we will study some of its components: stars, galaxies, the sun, comets, asteroids, natural satellites and planets. We will study things that we can observe with the naked eye and things that we need a **telescope** to see.

unassisted vision

Now we will learn about the stars and galaxies.

The Stars

These are celestial bodies that emit light. Stars have different temperatures, which is why they appear to be different colors, like violet, blue, red, yellow and white.

Word Focus

Celestial bodies are the objects that form part of the universe.

Did You Know...?

Since ancient times, humans have connected the stars with imaginary lines to make figures called **constellations**. Two well-known examples are the Big Bear and Orion, or the Hunter, whose belt is formed by three stars called the Three Marias.

Have you seen any constellations? Which ones? Go to **Activity Card 6** to play a game with the constellations.

The Galaxies

Billions of **galaxies** make up the universe. They each contain cosmic dust and millions of stars, planets and gases that interact with each other and **orbit** around a common point. Andromeda and the Milky Way are examples of galaxies.

Scientists classify galaxies according to their shape. They can be spiral, lenticular, elliptical or irregular.

Earth is located in a spiral galaxy called the **Milky Way**. The Milky Way belongs to a group of galaxies called the **Local Group**, which is composed of approximately 30 galaxies.

Word Focus

To **orbit** is to travel around something, like a moon around a planet, in a curved path.

Can you see the Milky Way from Earth?

Let's Practice

1. What are some of the components of the universe? Name

____

____

Let's Summarize

The origin of the ____________________ can be explained by a huge explosion known as the ____________________.

Stars are ____________________ that emit light.

Galaxies contain ____________________, ____________________ and ____________________, among other components.

The Solar System

Let's Connect

The **solar system** is composed of a main star, the sun, and smaller components like comets, asteroids, natural satellites and planets.

Can you think of any celestial bodies in the solar system? Discuss.

Fun Fact!

Meteoroids are pieces of rock that have broken loose from the tails of comets or asteroids. When they enter Earth's atmosphere, they become **meteors**, commonly called **shooting stars**. When a meteoroid reaches the surface of the planet, it is called a **meteorite**.

1 The **sun** is a small, medium-aged star. It is orbited by the planets and other celestial bodies of the solar system. It is also our main source of light and heat.

2 **Comets** are celestial bodies made of rock and ice that orbit the sun.

3 **Asteroids** are made of rock and are smaller than a planet. They orbit the sun.

4 **Natural satellites** are celestial bodies that orbit planets. They are commonly known as moons. Our moon, Jupiter's Ganymede and Mars's Phobos are examples.

5 **Planets** are celestial bodies that do not emit their own light but reflect the light of the sun. They also orbit around the sun.

What planets are in the solar system? Talk with a classmate.

Did You Know...?

Haley's Comet is so big it can be seen from Earth with the naked eye. Its orbit around the sun takes about 75–76 years.

Fun Fact!

Artificial satellites are objects put into orbit by humans. There are more than 2,400 artificial satellites orbiting Earth!

Let's Practice

1. Describe two components of the solar system. Describe

____

____

Let's Summarize

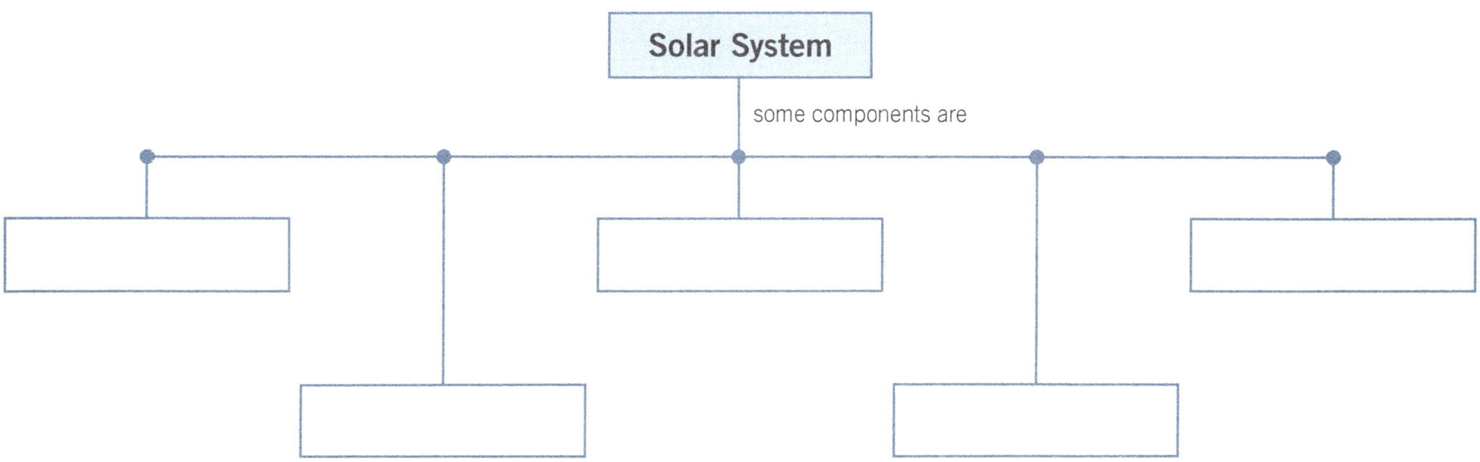

The Planets

Let's Connect

There are eight known planets in the solar system today. In order from the closest to the sun to the farthest, they are: Mercury, Venus, Earth, Mars, Jupiter, Saturn, Uranus and Neptune.

The planets can be classified as **interior planets** (those closest to the sun) and **exterior planets** (those farthest from the sun).

The Interior Planets

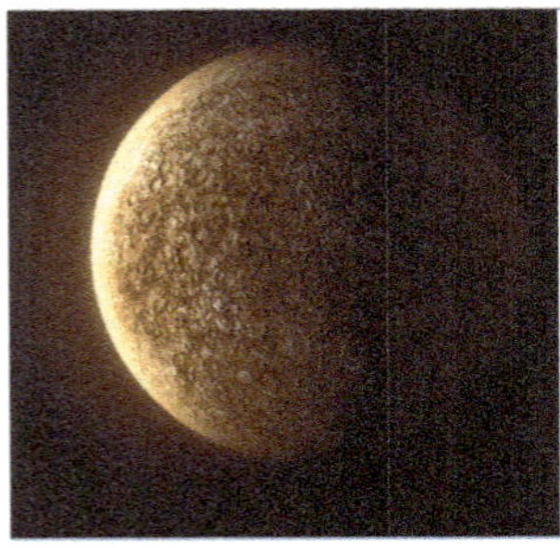

Mercury

- The first planet and the one closest to the sun.
- It does not have any natural satellites.
- It takes approximately 88 days to circle or orbit the sun.
- Its day lasts 1,406 hours.

Venus

- The second planet and the one closest to Earth.
- It is known as the morning star or evening star as it is often seen at sunrise or sunset.
- It does not have any natural satellites.
- It takes approximately 225 days to orbit the sun.
- Its day lasts 243 Earth days, and it rotates in the opposite direction from the other planets.

Earth

- The third planet and the only one known to support life.
- It has one natural satellite called the moon.
- It takes approximately 365 days to orbit the sun.
- Its day lasts 24 hours.

Mars

- The fourth planet, known as the red planet.
- It has two natural satellites: Phobos and Deimos.
- It takes approximately 687 days to orbit the sun.
- Its day lasts approximately 25 hours.

The Exterior Planets

Jupiter

- The fifth planet, and the largest in the solar system.
- Currently 67 natural satellites have been identified. The largest and best-known are Ganymede, Callisto, Io and Europa.
- It takes approximately 12 years to orbit the sun.
- Its day lasts approximately 10 hours.

Saturn

- The sixth planet and the second largest in the solar system. It has large rings.
- It has 62 confirmed natural satellites.
- It takes approximately 29 years to orbit the sun.
- Its day lasts 10 hours.

Uranus

- The seventh planet and the third largest in the solar system. It rotates on its side.
- It has 27 confirmed natural satellites.
- It takes approximately 165 years to orbit the sun.
- Its day lasts approximately 17 hours.

Neptune

- The eighth planet.
- It has 13 recognized natural satellites.
- It takes approximately 165 years to orbit the sun.
- Its day lasts approximately 15 days.

There are other celestial bodies in the solar system that orbit the sun called **dwarf planets**. Some dwarf planets recognized by the International Astronomical Union are **Pluto**, **Ceres** and **Eris**.

Let's Practice

1. Go to **Cutout 8** on **page 167**. Glue the planets according to size from the smallest to the largest. Write their names below. Put in order

2. Use the information from the previous pages to answer. Compare and contrast

a. Which is bigger, Earth or Jupiter?

b. Which planet takes longer to orbit the sun, Venus or Saturn?

c. Circle the interior planets in blue and the exterior planets in red.

Let's Summarize

Currently there are eight known planets in the solar system. In order from the closest to the sun to the farthest, they are: ____________, ____________, ____________, ____________, ____________, ____________, ____________ and ____________.

Quiz Yourself

1. Make a mobile of the solar system. You will need nine balls of different sizes, two sticks approximately 50 cm long, string, tape and a pen. If you can, find a motor from a small electronic device.

- Paint the balls according to the characteristics of the different planets and the sun.
- Make a cross with the sticks, as seen in the picture.
- Cut nine pieces of string of equal length and tape each one to a ball.
- Hang the ball that represents the sun at the point where the two sticks cross.
- Place the planets according to their distances from the sun.
- Cut four pieces of string of equal length and tie them to the ends of the sticks.
- Join the strings at the same point. Use the picture to help. If you have a motor, attach it now.
- Your solar system mobile is now ready!

2. What are the characteristics of the following components of the universe? Name at least two.

a. Galaxies: • ____________________

• ____________________

b. Stars: • ____________________

• ____________________

c. Comets: • ____________________

• ____________________

Section 2

The Movements of Earth

The Rotation of Earth

Let's Explore

1. Find a coin and a top. First **spin** the coin. Then spin the top.
   a. How do the objects spin? Describe

   ____

   b. When you watch these objects, what do they have in common? Compare

   ____

What movements do you observe? Discuss with a classmate.

Earth, like the coin and the top, spins on its own axis of rotation, which is an imaginary line that passes through Earth from pole to pole. This movement is known as rotation.

Rotation is the spinning of an object on its axis or central point, like Earth does.

Earth takes about **24 hours** to make one complete rotation on its axis, which is commonly known as an Earth day. In addition, our planet spins from **west** to **east**. This is why we see the sun in the east in the morning and in the west at night.

Word Focus

The **axis of rotation** is an imaginary line that connects the **North Pole** with the **South Pole**.

▲ Representation of the rotation of Earth.

Did you know that Earth's axis of rotation is tilted?

tilted → inclined

Let's Practice

2. With a partner, find a flashlight, a clay or Styrofoam ball and a skewer with the ends cut off.

– Ask your teacher to insert the skewer into the ball, as in the picture.

– Turn on the flashlight and point it at the ball from one spot. Have your partner hold the skewer at an angle.

a. Which components of the solar system do the objects represent? Relate

Flashlight: ____________________

Ball: ____________________

Skewer: ____________________

b. Does the flashlight illuminate the entire ball? What do the parts in light and shadow represent? Describe

____

____

c. If you spin the ball on the skewer, what happens to the area of light on the ball? Explain. Explain

____

____

Let's Summarize

Rotation occurs when ____________________.

This movement takes about ____________________, which corresponds to one ____________________.

Earth spins on its ____________________.

The Effects of Earth's Rotation

Let's Connect

As you have learned, Earth is constantly spinning on its axis. But does this movement have an effect on the planet? It does! The main effect is that it produces **day** and **night**.

This spinning of Earth causes one half of the planet to receive light from the sun and the other to receive no light. When an area has light, it is called **daytime**. When an area does not have light, it is called **nighttime**.

The rotation of Earth lasts 24 hours. In general, there are 12 hours of day and 12 hours of night.

This happens near the equator, where the day and the night have approximately the same duration. If you are farther away from the equator, the duration of the night and day varies according to the season.

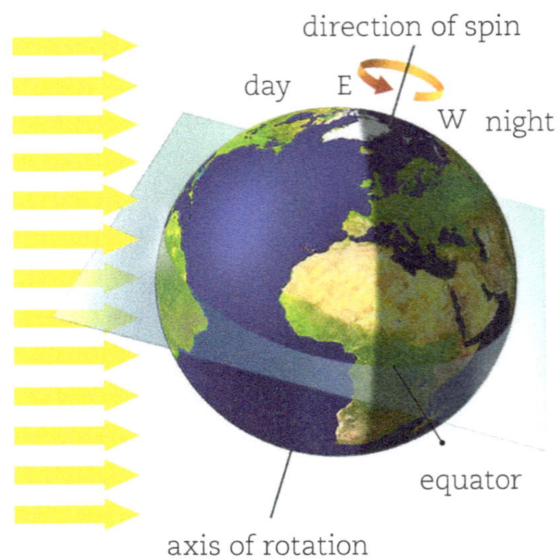

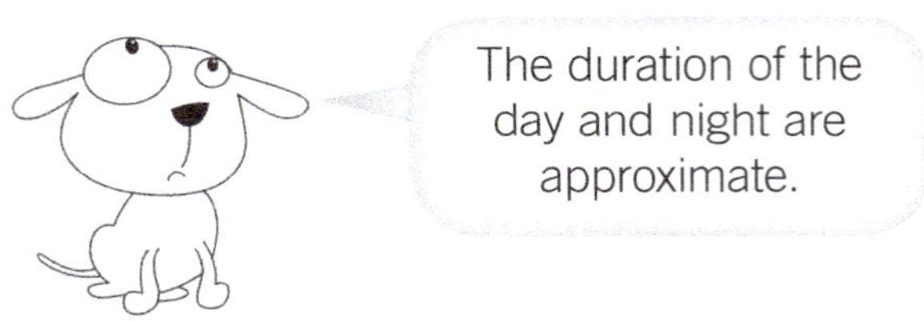

1. Use what you have learned to answer the questions. Infer

a. Would we have day and night if Earth did not spin on its axis?

____

____

b. What would happen to the day and night if the rotation of Earth lasted 12 hours?

____

____

Fun Fact!

Earth is shaped like a **geoid**. This means it is flatter at the poles and wider at the equator. Its rotation is one of the reasons Earth is shaped like this.

Let's Practice

2. You need a globe and a flashlight to do the following activity.

– Shine your light on your country.

– Slowly begin to turn the globe until your country cannot be seen.

– Keep turning the globe until your country returns to the area with light.

a. The light from the flashlight represents sunlight in this activity. Draw how the light hit Earth in each situation. Represent

Tip

Hold the flashlight in the same position for each step, or your results will be inaccurate.

b. Why is it daytime in your country? Explain

____

c. If it is daytime in your country, in which country is it nighttime? Predict

____

Let's Summarize

The main effect of Earth's rotation is ______________________________.

Earth takes ______________ to spin. As Earth rotates, one half receives light from the sun. In this half, it is ______________. When an area does not receive light from the sun, it is called ______________. Night and day last approximately ______________.

The Orbital Revolution of Earth

Let's Connect

1. Look at the picture.

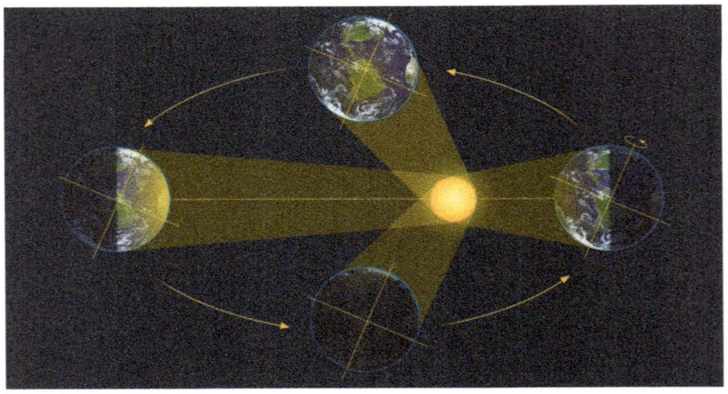

a. Is Earth always in the same position in relation to the sun? Why or why not? Infer

As the picture above shows, our planet doesn't stay in one place; it revolves around the sun. Its position relative to the sun changes every 365 days, 5 hours and 49 minutes, which is one year on Earth. This movement is known as orbital revolution.

Orbital revolution is when an object rotates around an external point. It is another way to describe how Earth moves around the sun.

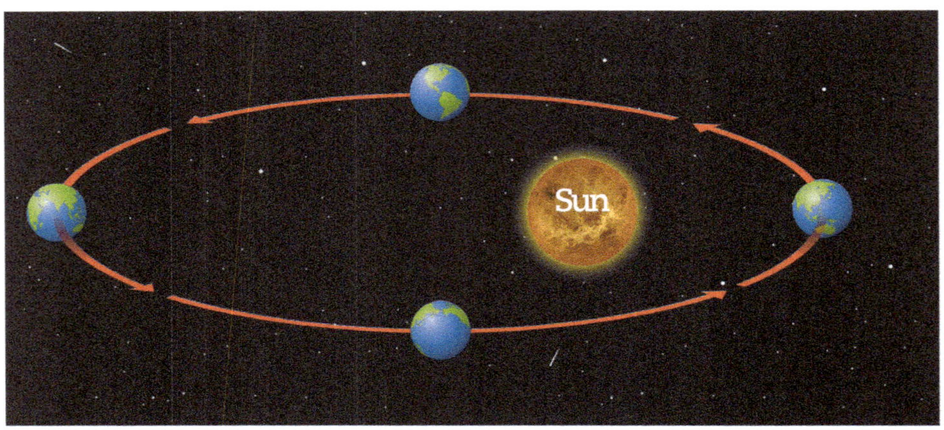

▲ Earth orbiting the sun.

Challenge

With a partner, use your bodies to demonstrate the difference between rotation and orbital revolution.

Every planet orbits a star, like our sun.

The Effects of Earth's Orbital Revolution

spring

summer

fall/autumn

winter

What are the similarities and differences between the pictures above? They show the same location during different **seasons of the year**. The seasons are a consequence of Earth's orbital revolution and its tilted axis of rotation. These things cause light from the sun to shine with different **intensity** on the various areas of Earth during different seasons.

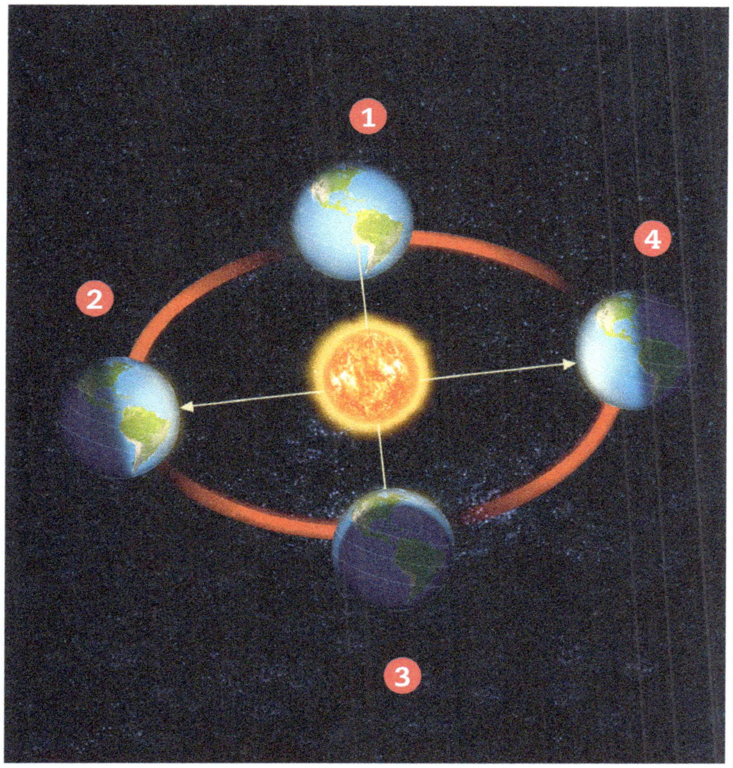

1. **March Equinox**. Earth is in an **intermediate** or a halfway position. Light from the sun falls with greater intensity on the equator.
2. **June Solstice**. At this time, it is summer in the northern hemisphere, which is tilted toward the sun and therefore receives a greater intensity of sunlight. The southern hemisphere, where it is winter, receives a lower intensity of sunlight.
3. **September Equinox**. Earth is in an intermediate or a halfway position, similar to the March Equinox. Light from the sun falls with greater intensity on the equator.
4. **December Solstice**. At this time, it is summer in the southern hemisphere, which is tilted toward the sun and therefore receives a greater intensity of sunlight. The northern hemisphere, where it is winter, receives a lower intensity of sunlight.

Did You Know...?

The day of the solstice is either the longest day of the year (in the summer) or the shortest (in the winter) for all places except those on the equator, which receive 12 hours of sunlight all through the year.

Let's Practice

2. How does Earth move around the sun? Let's find out. You will need a piece of white poster paper, a marker, a globe and a flashlight. Experiment

- Draw the orbit of Earth on the paper, as in the picture.
- Place the flashlight in the center of the orbit.
- Put the globe on the orbit line. Observe which area is illuminated.
- Start to slowly move the globe along the orbit. Make sure to keep the axis tilted at the same angle.
- Observe how sunlight, represented by the flashlight, falls on each hemisphere of the globe. Is it equally intense for all areas? Which hemisphere receives more intense sunlight?
- Continue moving the globe until one revolution has been completed. Closely observe how each hemisphere is illuminated.
- Divide the paper into four sections. Move the globe along the orbit line again. Find the points that correspond to the equinoxes and solstices.

3. What causes the change of seasons? Describe

____

____

____

____

Let's Summarize

The main effects of Earth's ____________________ and its ____________________ axis of ______________ are the ________________.

Quiz Yourself

1. Look at the picture.

a. Which movement of Earth is represented?

b. What are the effects of this movement of Earth? Explain one.

2. Use the following representation to answer.

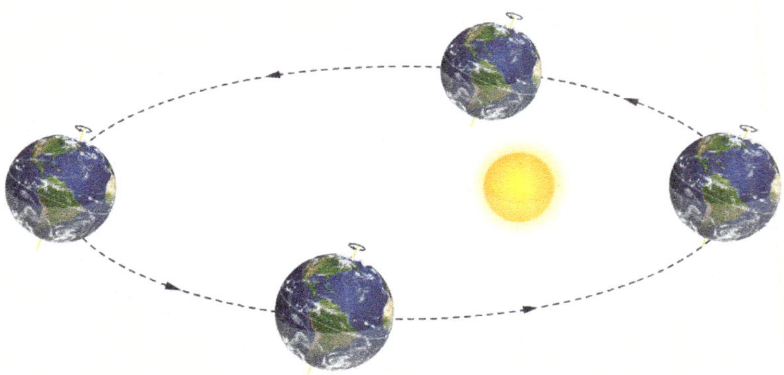

a. Which movement of Earth is represented?

b. When it is summer in your country, where is it winter?

c. Explain the difference in sunlight during the different seasons.

Let's Check!

1. Match each solar system component with its description.

comets	Celestial bodies like the moon and Phobos that orbit a planet.
asteroids	The main source of light and heat, and the body that the planets in the solar system orbit.
planets	Rocky bodies that are smaller than a planet and orbit the sun.
the sun	Celestial bodies mainly made of rock and ice.
natural satellites	Celestial bodies that orbit and reflect the light of the sun.

2. Draw the components of the solar system in their correct locations.

Solar System

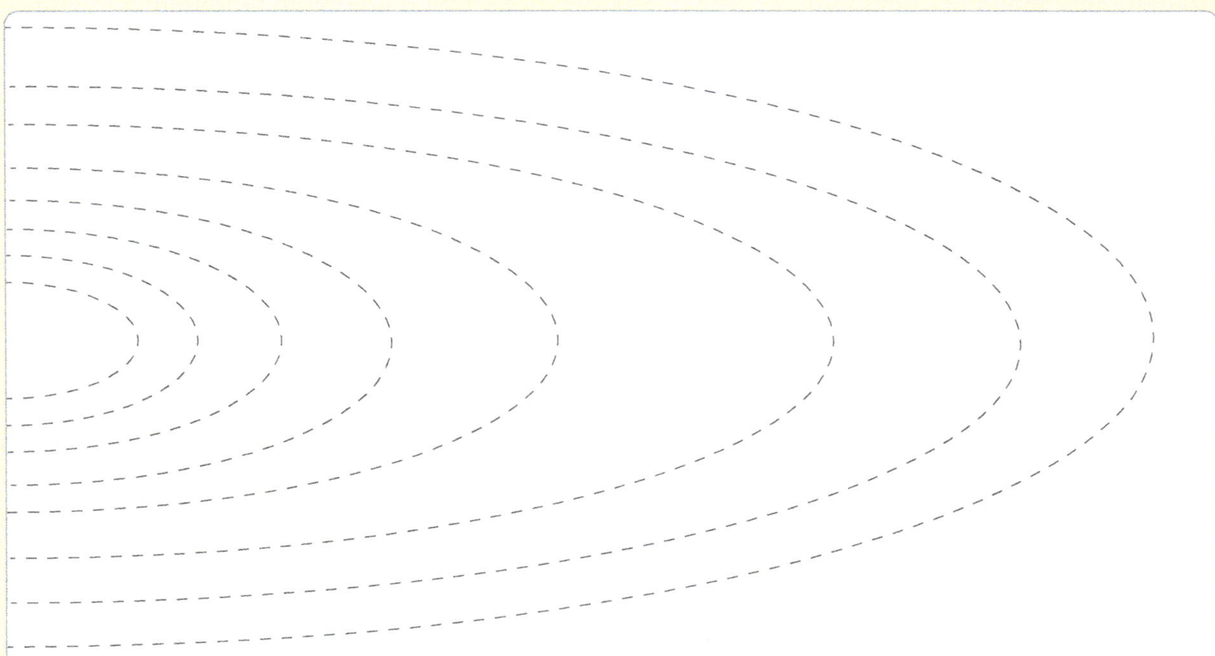

3. Write one similarity and one difference between the movements of Earth.

	Rotation	Orbital Revolution
Difference		
Similarity		

4. What are the main effects of the movements of Earth?

Type of Movement	Effects

How Did You Do?

For each ☺ color a ⬭.

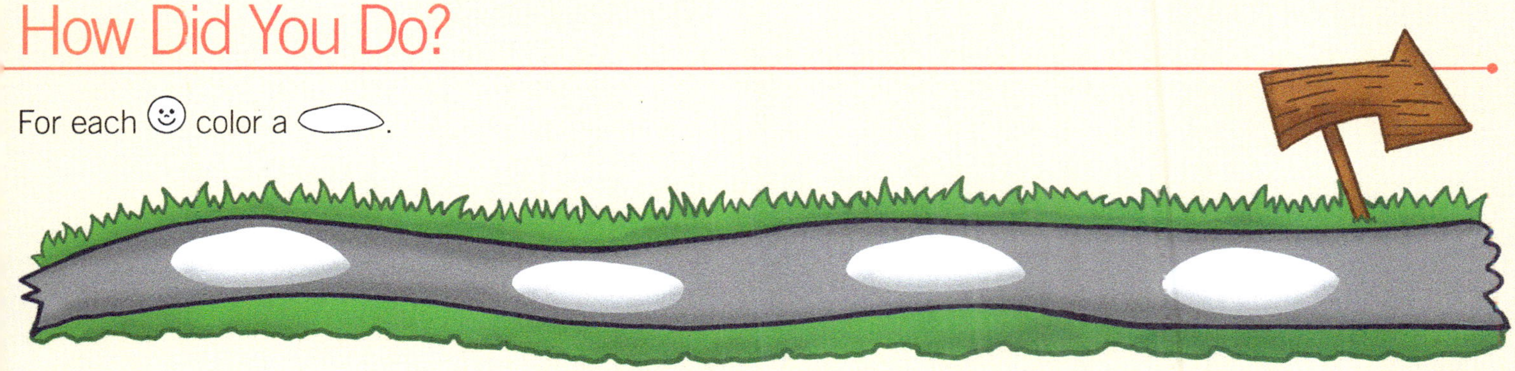

Solar System Events

The Phases of the Moon

Let's Connect

Do you know how many natural satellites Earth has? Earth's only natural satellite is the moon, which is an illuminated body because it reflects the light from the sun. The moon **orbits** Earth and takes 28 days to complete one **lunar cycle**. It also spins on its own axis of rotation, and one complete revolution takes 28 days.

It can be observed that the area of the moon illuminated by the sun changes according to the position of the sun, the moon and Earth. This is why we say the moon has **phases**. Some phases are: **new moon**, **waning crescent**, **full moon** and **waxing crescent**.

New moon. In this phase, the sun illuminates the hidden or far side of the moon, which is why it is not seen from Earth.

Full moon. In this phase, the sun illuminates the visible face of the moon. The whole moon is visible from Earth.

Waxing crescent. In this phase, the sun illuminates the lateral part of the moon, forming a C shape. The illuminated part gets bigger day by day.

Waning crescent. In this phase, the sun illuminates the side of the moon, forming a D shape. The illuminated part gets smaller day by day.

Did You Know...?

It takes the moon the same amount of time to orbit Earth as it does to complete one rotation on its axis, which is why we always see the same side of the moon.

Let's Practice

1. Choose a day of the week and observe the moon on the same day for one month.

a. Go to **Cutout 9** on **page 169**. Glue the phases of the moon below according to your observations. Identify

Week 1	Week 2	Week 3	Week 4

b. Does the moon look the same during the month? Recognize ☐ yes ☐ no

c. Why did the moon look different? Apply

____

d. Which phases of the moon do you recognize? Identify

Week 1: ______________________________

Week 2: ______________________________

Week 3: ______________________________

Week 4: ______________________________

Let's Summarize

The moon is the only ____________ satellite of ____________. It takes the moon ______ days to rotate on its axis and the same amount of time to orbit ____________.

Different areas of the moon, known as phases, are illuminated according to the positions of the ____________, the ____________ and ____________.

Some commonly known phases are: ______________________________.

Eclipses

Let's Explore

1. With a partner, find a globe, a flashlight and a balloon.

   – Blow up the balloon, and place it in front of the globe.
   – One person should line up the flashlight, the balloon and the globe, as in the picture.
   – Shine the flashlight toward the balloon and observe what happens.

   a. Which areas are illuminated? Which are dark? Observe

   ____

   ____

As you learned, Earth and the moon are constantly moving. This movement creates special events in the solar system. One of these events is an **eclipse**, which happens when the **shadow** of one body falls upon another body, making it dark.

Eclipses are common events in the solar system. In the case of our planet, we experience **eclipses of the sun and moon**, known as solar and lunar eclipses.

Education through Values

When you work as a team, you should listen to the opinions and ideas of every member. This shows respect for your teammates.

Did You Know...?

Conjunctions are solar system events when the planets form a line. **Lesser conjunctions** occur when the interior planets line up on the same side of the sun. **Superior conjunctions** occur when the sun is located between the planets.

Let's Practice

2. Use the previous experiment to answer.
   a. Draw what you observed on **Activity Card 7**. Include the illuminated and nonilluminated areas. Describe
   b. Why are there areas without light on the globe? Infer

   ____

   ____

   c. What would happen if you placed the globe between the balloon and the flashlight? Predict

   ____

3. What is an eclipse? Explain

____

____

4. Andy placed a soccer ball between a flashlight and the wall.
   a. What do you think he will see on the wall? Predict

   ____

   ____

   b. Which solar system event is being represented? Identify

   ☐ eclipse ☐ phases of the moon

Let's Summarize

Eclipses occur when ______________________________

______________________________.

Eclipses on our planet are ______________________________ and

______________________________.

Lunar and Solar Eclipses

Let's Connect

Lunar eclipses occur when Earth is between the sun and the moon. In this case, Earth blocks the light from the sun and projects a shadow on the moon. Since the moon is not illuminated, it cannot be seen from Earth.

The shadow that Earth projects is divided into two parts. They are:

– **umbra**, the darkest part of the shadow.

– **penumbra**, the least dark part of the shadow.

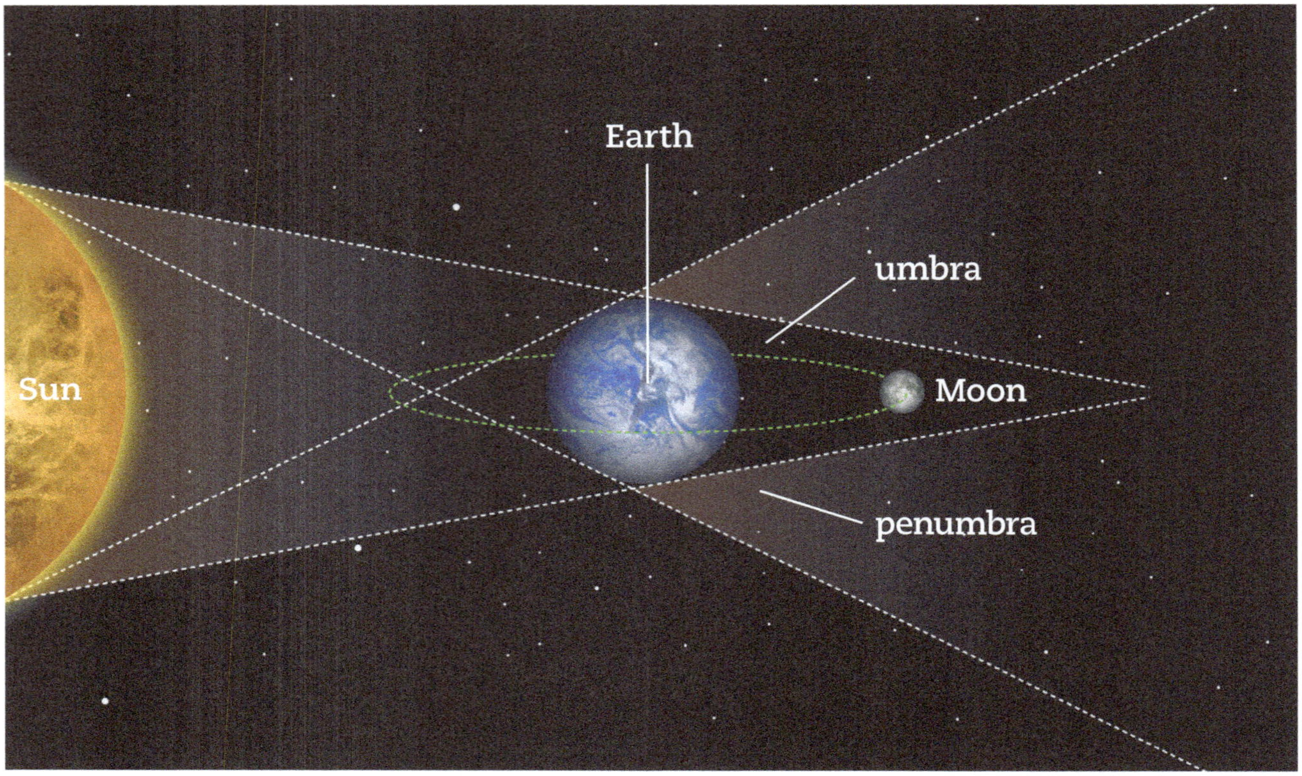

There are two types of lunar eclipses.

If the moon is located in the umbra, it is called a **total eclipse**.

If the moon is located in the penumbra, it is called a **partial eclipse**.

Solar eclipses occur when the moon is between the sun and Earth, effectively covering the sun completely.

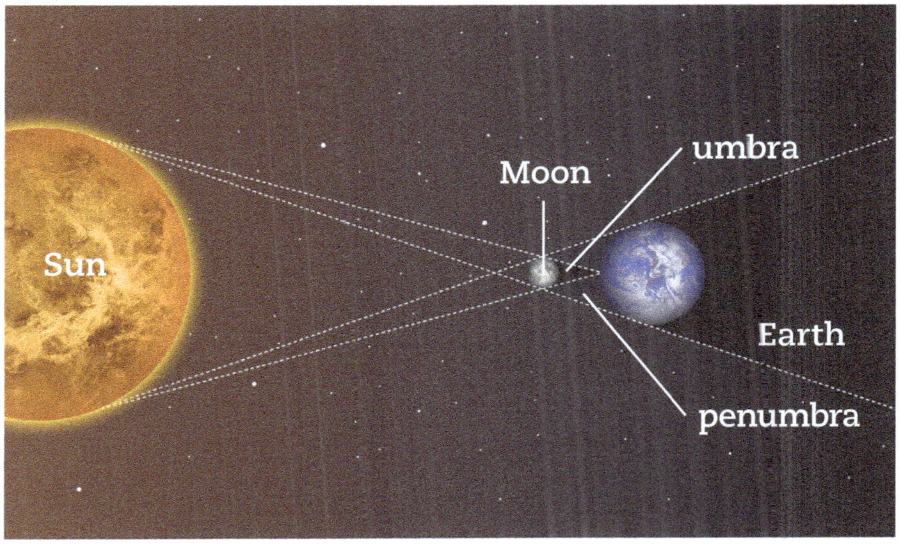

There are three types of solar eclipses: **partial eclipse**, **annular eclipse** and **total eclipse**.

Partial eclipse

The moon does not totally cover the sun. It looks like a crescent and creates a small cone of shadow.

Annular eclipse

The moon does not completely cover the sun. This depends on how close the moon is to Earth at the time of the eclipse—if it is close, a total eclipse is more likely.

probable

Total eclipse

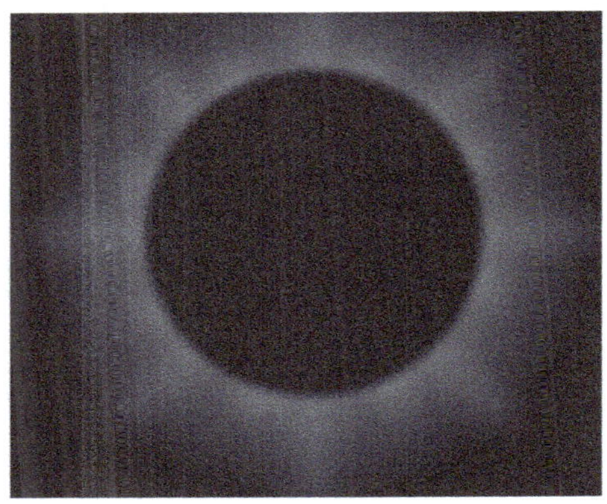

The moon completely covers the sun and creates a large cone of shadow that is projected toward Earth.

Staying Healthy

Eclipses are fascinating events to observe, especially solar eclipses. However, to observe them safely, you must take certain precautions, like using special glasses and never looking directly at the sun.

Let's Practice

1. Look at the lunar calendar. Answer the questions.

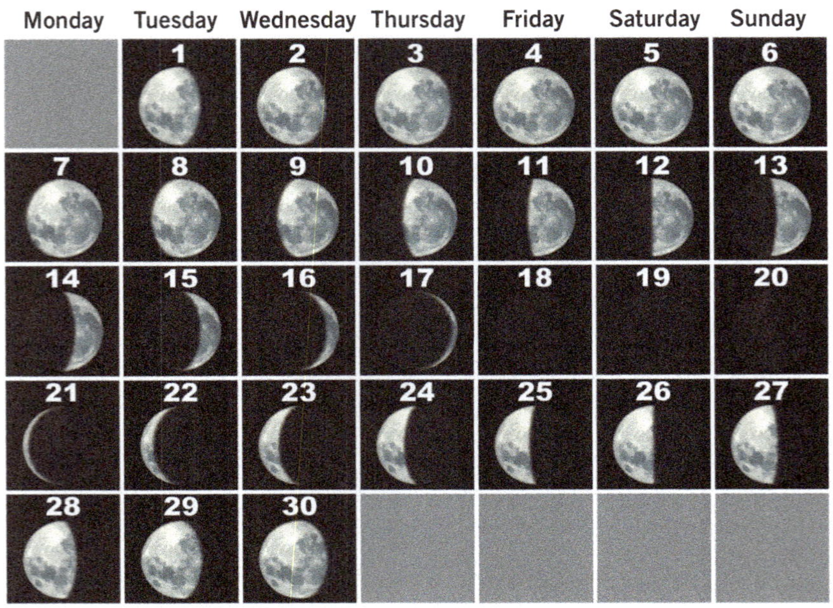

a. On which days will the moon not be seen? Identify

____

____

b. When is the next **full moon**? Predict

____

____

2. Mark the solar eclipse with a ✔ (blue) and the lunar eclipse with a ✔ (orange). Identify

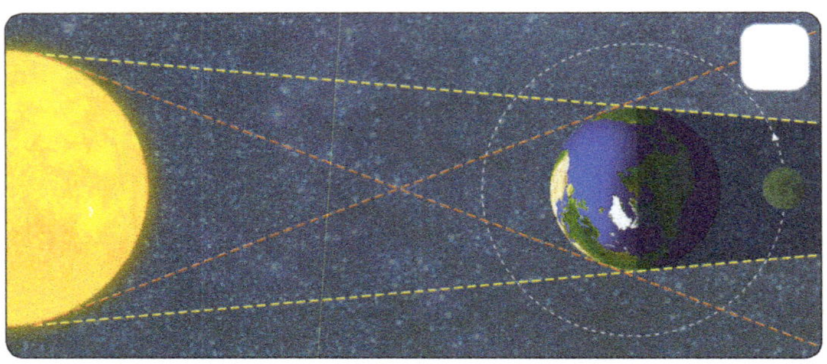

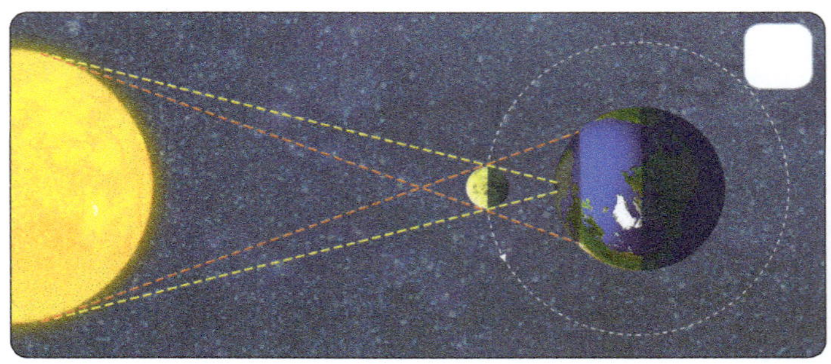

Let's Summarize

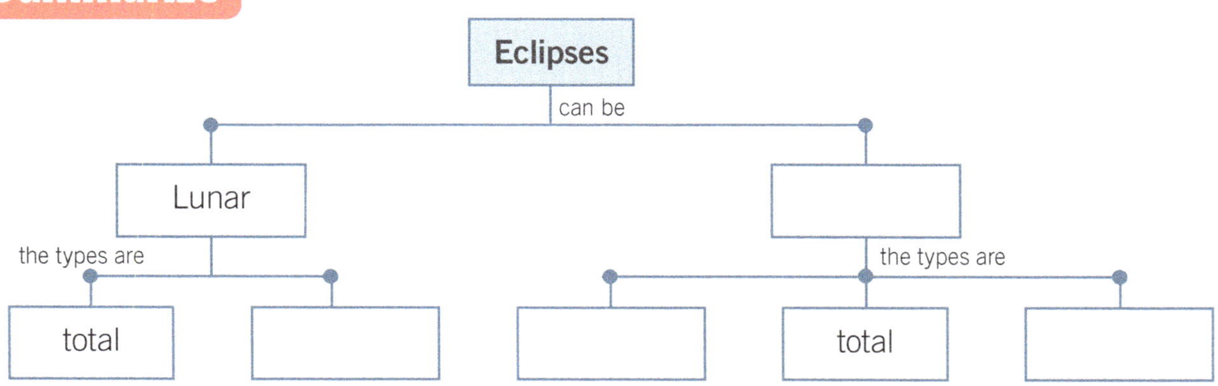

Quiz Yourself

1. Look at the picture and answer.

a. How would you place the spheres to represent an eclipse? Draw.

b. What type of eclipse did you make? Explain.

____

2. How can you represent an eclipse? You will need two spheres, one smal and the other medium-sized, and a small flashlight.

- Place the spheres on the ground 15 cm apart.
- Place the flashlight approximately 15 cm from the medium-sized sphere.
- Turn on the flashlight. Observe the effect of the light on the sphere.
- Switch the positions of the spheres. Raise the small sphere a little in order to center the shadow on the bigger sphere.

a. What does the flashlight represent in the experiment? Mark with a ✔.

☐ the moon ☐ the sun ☐ Earth

b. What does the small sphere represent? ______________________.

c. What does the large sphere represent? ______________________.

Does the Moon Have Different Shapes during a Month?

Basic Framework

The moon orbits Earth and also rotates on its own axis. The cycle of the moon is 28 days.

Observation

Look at the pictures.

1. What celestial body do you see?

____

2. How are the pictures different?

____

____

Research Question

Why does the shape of the moon seem to change?

Hypothesis

The shape of the moon changes because different areas are in shadow.

Predictions

1. If one side of a ball is painted and placed in front of the sun, what will you see? Draw.

2. If the ball is placed in front of the sun but observed from a different position, what do you think you will see?

____

____

____

____

Experimental Procedure

Supplies

A Styrofoam ball, a skewer, a black marker and a pencil.

Steps

1. Color half of the ball with the black marker.
2. Form a circle. One student holds the ball.
3. One student observes from the center while the others pass the ball around. Make sure not to rotate the ball.
4. Change positions so that everyone has a turn to observe from the center.

Results

1. Draw what the ball looked like when you were in the center of the circle. Compare your drawing with your classmates' drawings.

Position 1	Position 2	Position 3	Position 4

2. What celestial body does the ball represent? What does the person in the center represent?

Conclusions

1. What solar system event is represented in this experiment? Explain.

2. Communicate your observations using a drawing or chart. Use **Activity Card 8**.
3. Compare your drawing with your classmates' drawings.

transmit

To communicate is to relay your observations through a drawing, chart or other manner. **To compare**, you should focus on the similarities and differences between your observations and those of your classmates.

What Did You Learn?

1. What makes the sun different from the planets?

____

____

Mark the correct answers with a ✔.

2. Which of the following statements describe comets?

A. Celestial bodies that emit light.

B. Celestial bodies that orbit the sun.

C. Rocky bodies that orbit a planet.

D. Celestial bodies made of rock and ice.

3. The movements of Earth produce:

A. Solar and lunar eclipses.

B. Eclipses and the day and night.

C. Cloudy days and seasons.

D. Day and night and seasons.

4. Draw a lunar eclipse. Describe it.

____

____

Scientific Skill: Communicate and compare

5. With two partners, find a tennis ball, a basketball and a lamp. Ask your partner to hold the tennis ball between the lamp and the basketball. Turn on the lamp and observe what happens. Next, place the basketball between the lamp and the tennis ball.

a. What differences did you see between the two situations?

____

____

b. What phenomena are represented in this experiment?

____

____

c. Draw what you observed in the first situation.

Draw a solar eclipse and hang it on your class bulletin board.

How Did You Do?

For each ☺ color a ⬭.

Find Test 5 Study Page

Glossary

3.1 Key Words Unit 1

native – *adj*, originally belonging to or coming from

life cycle – *n*, the series of stages a living thing passes through

reproduce – *v*, to produce young; to breed

pollinate – *v*, to carry pollen from the male part of a flower to the female part of the same or another flower

crop – *n*, a plant that people grow on farms, usually for food

3.2 Key Words Unit 2

garbage – *n*, waste material that is thrown away

conserve – *v*, to keep and protect from damage, loss or change

resource – *n*, something useful or helpful for a particular purpose

organic – *adj*, relating to or coming from living things

inorganic – *adj*, relating to substances that come from minerals, as opposed to organic substances, which come from plants or animals

3.3 Key Words Unit 3

illness – *n*, the condition of being unwell or in poor health; a disease

healthy – *adj*, having or showing good health

unhealthy – *adj*, not having or showing good health; not fit or well

hygiene – *n*, cleanliness necessary for good health and to prevent disease

diet – *n*, the food and drink that a person or animal usually eats

3.4 Key Words Unit 4

vibrate – *v*, to move or to cause to move quickly back and forth; to shake or cause to shake

illuminate – *v*, to light up; to provide with light

ray – *n*, a narrow beam of light, heat or other form of radiant energy

sound – *n*, something that you can hear; vibrations that travel through the air that you can hear when they reach your eardrum

light – *n*, a form of radiation or energy that stimulates the organs of sight and makes things visible

3.5 Key Words Unit 5

universe – *n*, the whole of space and everything that exists in it, such as stars, planets and energy

solar – *adj*, relating to the sun

lunar – *adj*, relating to the moon

axis – *n*, an imaginary line that an object rotates around

phase – *n*, a particular stage in a cycle

A

absorb – *v*, to draw in and soak up

abundant – *adj*, plentiful or more than enough

align – *v*, to place in order or form a line

aluminum – *n*, a silver-white metal that is easy to shape; the most abundant metal in the earth's crust

annular – *adj*, ring-shaped; circular

artificial – *adj*, created by humans, not natural

asteroid – *n*, a small, rocky body orbiting the sun

B

balanced – *adj*, fair or equal; having the same amount on both sides

beam – *n*, a ray of light

big bang – *n*, the gigantic explosion of a single mass of material that is thought to have caused the beginning of the universe

biodegradable – *adj*, capable of being decomposed by the sun or bacteria

blend – *v*, to liquefy and mix together

body – *n*, a separate object of distinct mass; the main part or structure of something

C

can – *n*, a metal container for storing foods or liquids

celestial – *adj*, relating to the sky

celestial body – *n*, a natural object visible in the sky

checkup – *n,* medical revision

comet – *n*, an object in space with a bright center and a long trail of light behind it—a comet travels around the sun and is made of ice, frozen gases and dust particles

composition – *n*, the makeup of something

compost – *n*, a mix of rotting leaves and vegetables added to soil to make it better for growing

conclude – *v*, to reach a decision after careful consideration; to bring to an end

conjunction – *n*, when the orbits of planets coincide to bring them into a line—inferior conjunctions occur when planets line up on the same side of the sun, and superior conjunctions occur when they line up with the sun between them

constellation – *n*, a group of stars that people think of as having a certain shape and that are named based on this shape

contagious – *adj*, easily passed to others

cosmic – *adj*, relating to the universe and outer space

D

decibel – *n*, a unit for measuring how loud sound is

decompose – *v*, to decay or rot

deep – *adj*, of a low-pitched sound

dent – *n*, an area that is lower than the parts around it after being hit or pushed in

depth – *n*, the distance downward or inward

deteriorate – *v*, to become progressively worse

disperse – *v*, to move in different directions, to spread apart

duration – *n*, the length of time that something continues

E

echo – *n*, the repetition of a sound caused when sound waves bounce off a hard surface

eclipse – *n*, an event that occurs when a planet, star or moon is hidden or partly hidden by another celestial body—an eclipse of the moon happens when Earth moves between it and the sun

efficient – *adj*, able to produce results or actions without wasted energy

emit – *v*, to send out, give off or produce

equinox – *n*, a time of year in March and September when both day and night are exactly 12 hours long

expired – *adj*, no longer valid after a period of time

exploit – *v*, to put to full use

F

fat – *n*, the soft flesh on people and animals that keeps them warm and stores energy

firm – *adj*, solid, not soft

formulate – *v*, to prepare in a methodical manner

frequency – *n*, 1. the number of times a sound wave is repeated in a period of time 2. the fact or condition of happening often 3. the number of times that something happens in a particular period

G

galaxy – *n*, a large group of stars held together by the force of gravitation

globe – *n*, a spherical representation of the earth

grind – *v*, to crush or break something into very small pieces using a machine or hard surface

H

habit – *n*, something a person does often and in the same way

handle – *v*, to manage, use or control with your hands

hertz – *n*, a unit used to measure the frequency of sound waves

high-pitched – *adj*, high in tone

honey – *n*, a thick, sweet substance made by bees

I

illuminate – *v*, to light up; to provide with light

incident ray – *n*, the ray of light that hits a surface

infection – *n*, a disease caused by germs entering the body

insulate – *v*, to add a material or substance to an object in order to stop heat, electricity or sound from going in or out of it

intensity – *n*, the quality or state of being intense

intermediate – *adj*, coming between two things; in the middle

intestine – *n*, an organ in the shape of a long tube that helps with digestion

L

landfill – *n*, a method of garbage disposal in which trash is buried with layers of soil above and below it

last – *v,* to endure, continue, persist

litter – *n*, trash such as paper, cans and bottles left in a public place; v, to leave trash in a public place

loud – *adj*, having a strong or intense sound; easy to hear

M

measure – *n*, an action planned or taken to produce a result; *v*, to find the size, length or amount of something

medium – *n*, the means or substance through which a thing travels or acts

meteor – *n*, a small body of stone or metal that enters Earth's atmosphere from space

meteorite – *n*, a meteor that has fallen to the ground without burning up completely

meteoroid – *n*, a small body in outer space that would become a meteor if it entered Earth's atmosphere

microorganism – *n*, an extremely small thing that can only be seen with a microscope

misuse – *v*, to use something in the wrong way or for the wrong reason

N

natural – *adj*, occurring in nature; not artificial

nonbiodegradable – *adj*, not capable of being decomposed naturally and therefore damaging to the environment

O

opaque – *adj*, not allowing light through, not transparent

orbit – *n*, the roughly circular path that a planet, moon or celestial body follows around another body

orbital revolution – *n*, a rotation around an external point

origin – *n*, the point or place where something begins, comes from or is created

P

partial – *adj*, not complete

pesticide – *n*, a chemical used to kill animals or insects that damage plants or crops

planet – *n*, a celestial body larger than an asteroid or a comet that orbits a star

pole – *n*, either of the two extreme points of the axis of Earth, called the North Pole and the South Pole

practice – *v*, to do something many times in order to become better at it

preserve – *v*, to protect from damage, loss or decay

prism – *n*, a transparent glass or crystal object that can separate a beam of light into the colors of the rainbow

propagate – *v*, to travel through a medium (usually light, sound and radio waves)

pulp – *n*, any soft, moist mixture of plant matter

R

recorder – *n*, a musical instrument shaped like a tube with holes and played by blowing into one end

recycle – *v*, to make something new from an old object or material

reduce – *v*, to cut down on; to decrease

reflected ray – *n*, the ray of light reflected by a surface

reflect – *v*, to bounce off

refract – *v*, to make light change direction when it enters a new medium at an angle

relay – *v*, to communicate or transmit

reuse – *v*, to use again

revolve – *v*, to move in a circle around a fixed object or point

rotate – *v*, to move in a circle around an axis

S

satellite – *n*, any body in space, such as a moon, that moves in orbit around another larger body, such as a planet

set – *v*, when the sun or another celestial body passes below the horizon

shadow – *n*, the figure or dark area of shade made when light is blocked by something

shiny – *adj*, having a bright or reflective appearance

slightly – *adv*, not much

sneeze – *v*, to suddenly force air out of your mouth and nose as a reaction to dust or an illness

soft – *adj*, not loud, harsh or irritating; gentle; not hard to the touch

solar system – *n*, the eight planets and their moons in orbit around the sun

solstice – *n*, a time of year in June and December when the sun reaches its highest or lowest point in the sky at noon, marked by the longest and shortest days of the year

source – *n*, point of origin, where something comes from

spectrum – *n*, the group of colors that a ray of white light can be separated into; the colors of the rainbow

spin – *v*, to turn or cause to turn around quickly; to twirl

spread – *v*, to put out or extend over a wide area

star – *n*, a huge mass of brightly burning gases in space

sunrise – *n*, the time in the morning that the sun rises above the horizon

sunset – *n*, the time in the evening that the sun falls below the horizon

synthetic – *adj*, formed by chemical reactions rather than found in nature; artificial, man-made

T

taut – *adj*, stretched tight; not loose

telescope – *n*, a tube-shaped instrument with powerful lenses that makes distant objects appear nearer and larger

tilt – *v*, to make something slope or lean by raising one end

tone – *n*, the quality and character of a sound

total – *adj*, including everything; making up the whole; entire

translucent – *adj*, not transparent, but clear enough for some light to pass through

transmit – *v*, to send or pass information

transparent – *adj*, completely clear; allowing light to pass through so that objects behind can be seen clearly

travel – *v*, to move from one place to another

U

utensil – *n*, a simple and useful device used for completing tasks

V

vibrate – *v*, to move continuously and rapidly back and forth

vibration – *n*, a rapid back and forth motion; trembling

W

weigh – *v*, to find out how heavy something is

whisper – *v*, to speak very softly under your breath

Cutout 1

Use on page 15 **(Unit 1)**.

Cutout 2

Use on page 33 **(Unit 1)**.

Cutout 3
Use on page 46 **(Unit 2)**.

Cutout 4
Use on page 72 **(Unit 3)**.

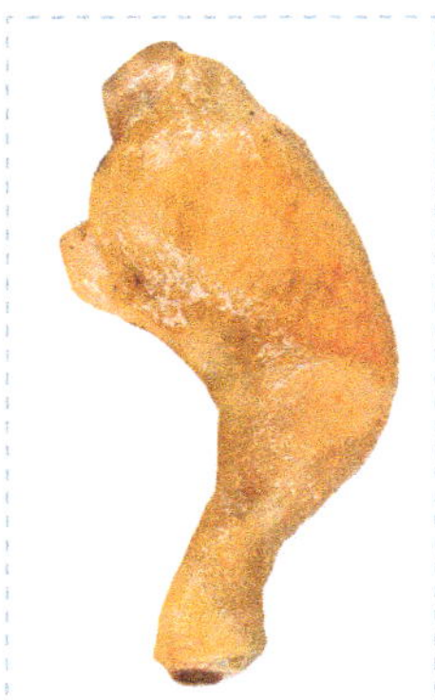

Cutouts

Cutout 5
Use on page 79 **(Unit 3)**.

Cutout 6
Use on page 91 **(Unit 4)**.

Cutout 7
Use on page 103 (**Unit 4**).

Cutouts

Cutout 8
Use on page 126 (**Unit 5**).

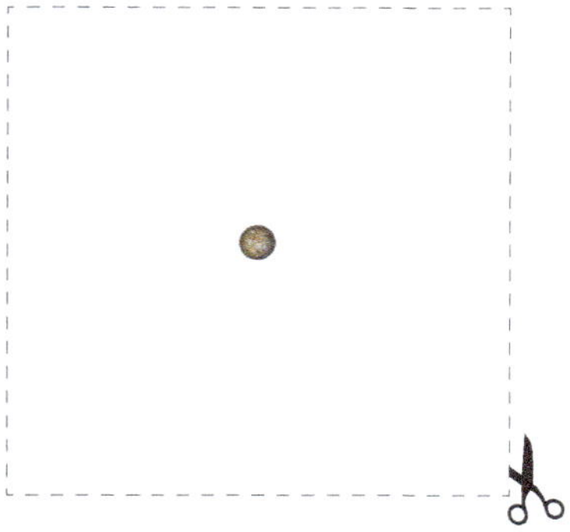

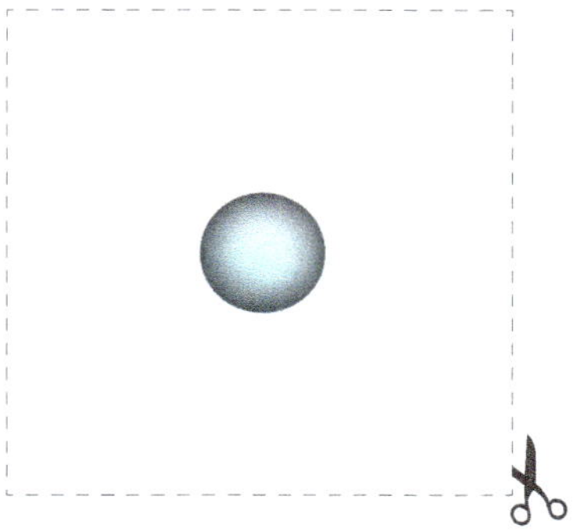
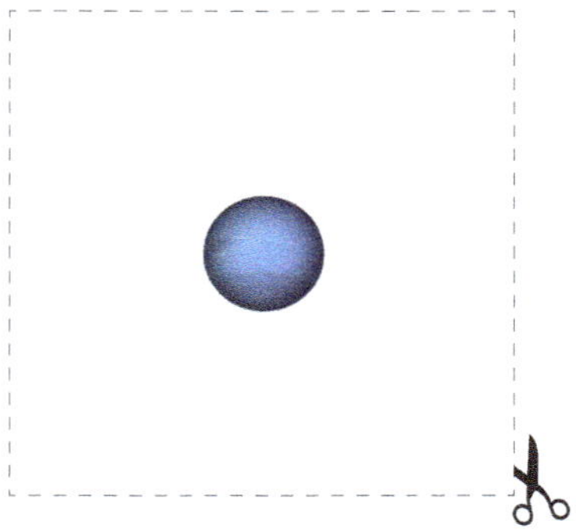

Cutout 9
Use on page 139 (**Unit 5**).